CHRISTIAN FAITH SERIES
REINHOLD NIEBUHR *Consulting Editor*

THE RENEWAL OF MAN

BOOKS BY ALEXANDER MILLER

The Renewal of Man
Biblical Politics: Studies in Christian Social Doctrine
Christian Faith and My Job
The Christian Significance of Karl Marx

THE RENEWAL

OF MAN

A Twentieth Century Essay on

Justification by Faith

BY ALEXANDER MILLER

Doubleday & Company, Inc., Garden City, New York, 1955

Library of Congress Catalog Card Number 55–5296

Copyright ©, 1955, by Alexander Miller
All Rights Reserved
Printed in the United States
At the Country Life Press, Garden City, N.Y.
First Edition

The selections from Brother to Dragons, *by Robert Penn Warren, are copyright, 1953, by Robert Penn Warren; reprinted by permission of Random House, Inc.*

The lines from A Sleep of Prisoners, *by Christopher Fry, are copyright, 1951, by Christopher Fry; reprinted by permission of Oxford University Press, Inc.*

The selection from Arrival and Departure, *by Arthur Koestler, is copyright, 1943, by the author; from* Darkness at Noon, *by Arthur Koestler, is copyright, 1941, by The Macmillan Company; reprinted by permission of The Macmillan Company.*

The lines from The Everlasting Mercy, *by John Masefield, are copyright, 1911, 1936, by the author; reprinted by permission of The Macmillan Company.*

The lines from the Preface to Modern Poetry and the Christian Tradition, *by Amos Wilder, are reprinted by permission of Charles Scribner's Sons.*

To M.M. and L.M.

Parents and Teachers

Introduction to Christian Faith Series

Professor Miller's volume is the first in a series of volumes devoted to the exposition of the meaning of the Christian faith. This series is designed to make the main outlines of the age-old faith meaningful to modern people. The studies are meant to be "popular" but not in the sense of reducing the dimension of the faith to terms which would make it obviously relevant to the characteristic credos of our era. They are designed in the first instance for laymen who cannot be expected to know, or to be interested in, the nice points of Christian doctrine; or to understand the frequently esoteric language of which theologians, as other learned men, avail themselves. Therefore the "shoptalk" of theology is scrupulously avoided. Explanations are given in terms of common currency, or they are translated into terms which will make the Christian affirmations relevant to the experience of ordinary men in our era.

But the thought behind the series does not assume that the debate between the Christian faith and our secular culture can be resolved merely by reducing the esoteric terms, which are foreign to the vocabulary of modernity. The series is prompted by the conviction that the Christian faith is frequently most relevant to the experience of modern men when it is most challenging to their cherished presuppositions about the nature of man, and about the ultimate reality to which man must relate himself, and about the strange drama of our history. Christianity has tried rather too desperately to accommodate itself to modernity. In its desperation it frequently sacrificed just those points in the Christian Gospel which would throw light on mysteries which modern learning left obscure.

Professor Miller's volume is ideally suited to be the first in this series of volumes, interpreting various aspects of the Christian faith; for he does not try to reduce the Christian faith to a dimension which would make it "credible" to the modern age. He, on the contrary, explicates its real genius and shows why it cannot fit the religious alternatives which Koestler defines in his *Yogi and the Commissar*. It is a religion of history and not a "spiritual" religion, which seeks to flee from history. It affirms life but it is critical of the self. It does not seek for escape from the body but it seeks for escape from the self. And yet it regards the power of self-concern as so persistent that it warns everyone against the illusion of moral perfection. It derives charity and humility from the knowledge of divine forgiveness to all men, both the righteous and the unrighteous.

The series of volumes will analyze various aspects of this faith which have been neglected in the effort to make it conform to the presuppositions of modern men about the nature of life and religion. This is not an effort at iconoclasm in religion nor a specific challenge to the old conformity of faith to culture. It is merely an effort to state the main outlines of a biblical faith which understands the unity of men in body and soul; the meaningfulness of human history and the great obscurities of meaning which must be clarified; which rejects all idolatries of ancient or modern days; which worships a majestic and mysterious God who transcends all temporal realities but whose character is "disclosed" in a particular drama of history which must be apprehended by faith. Most of these affirmations are scandalous to the modern mind which tries to interpret everything in terms of natural and rational coherence. Yet it is to those "who believe" both "wisdom and power," that is the source of understanding for this strange drama of human existence; and the source of the power to live joyfully and humbly in a life which can never be ideally "completed" or purged of its evil.

The present age though incredulous toward the chief affirmations of this faith, is bound to find it more relevant than previous ages, which conceived their own schemes of salvation. Our age is the inheritor of the confusion and the evil which proceeded precisely from these schemes of salvation.

We shall present the various facets of the biblical faith and their relevance to our contemporary problems in the succeeding volumes as follows:

Man's Knowledge of God by Professor William Wolf

This volume will explain what is meant by "revelation" and by the definitive revelation in Jesus Christ, in the Christian faith; and how this definitive self-disclosure of God is related to the disclosures of God which we have in nature, in conscience, and in the experience of other religions. Professor

Wolf also defines the relation of faith, which apprehends revelation, to the reason, which analyzes the structures and coher-
ences of existence.

Doing the Truth by Dean James A. Pike

This volume on Christian ethics deals with the ethical problems which Christianity shares with any view of human freedom but emphasizes the unique aspects of the Christian view
of our moral responsibility, particularly the new factors which
are introduced by the Christian view of man's sin and failure,
of God's forgiveness and mercy, of the grateful response of the
sinner to this mercy and of the expression of love through
gratitude. Dean Pike also considers the problem of the constant
elements in moral standards amid shifting historical circum-
stances.

The Strangeness of the Church by Professor Daniel Jenkins

Professor Jenkins deals with the strangeness of the Church,
which is on the one hand an obvious historical institution, subject to every relativity and corruption of history, but on the
other hand a community of grace acknowledging loyalty to a
God whose righteousness transcends all historical achievements and who enables the worshiping community to discern
the severity of His judgments and the kindness of His mercy.
Ideally the Church is therefore that locus in history where
everything in history is challenged and may be renewed if the
challenge is accepted contritely.

Hardness of Heart, a contemporary interpretation of the doctrine of sin by Professor Edmond Cherbonnier

Professor Cherbonnier compares the Christian doctrine of sin with alternative explanations of historical evil and shows how integrally the Christian doctrine is related to the Christian estimate of man's freedom; and how relevant this interpretation is to the understanding of any current problem of human behavior.

In every study the Christian faith is presented, not as some historical remnant which is apologetically presented to the modern man, but as a unique approach to every problem of human nature and historical destiny, which will illumine what various aspects of modern culture have left obscure.

Contents

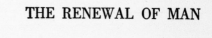

THE RENEWAL OF MAN

What honesty?
Not to say we do
A thing for all men's sake when we do it only
For our own. And quick eyes to see
Where evil is. While any is our own
We use fine words unsoundly. . . .

Who's to lead us out of this?
It's hard to see.

CHRISTOPHER FRY *A Sleep of Prisoners*

1. Man at the End of His Tether

We adapt a chapter title from H. G. Wells's last book, *Mind at the End of Its Tether*, in which he radically qualified his earlier rational and revolutionary optimism, and confessed himself perplexed, almost unto despair. He is not the only rationalist of his generation who has made good Christian copy by confessing to a new and wholesome helplessness in the face of contemporary crisis: though not all of them have sold out to the pious so completely as Bertrand Russell, who has been known to end his lectures of late with a coy reference to "that dirty word, Love," and has even gone so far as to drag in *"Christian* love" as a viable option for a repentant rationalist. The Christians ought not to count too much on this, but it is true that the temper of the times has changed. When I was an undergraduate, back in predepression days, those of us who breathed deep of the intellectual air of our time breathed a very skeptical air indeed. Bernard Shaw was a staple, and while he did go in for a tongue-in-cheek piety, especially when talking to rationalists, he could not be called a bulwark of classical Christianity. Aldous Huxley was a long way from his present esoteric piety, the younger C. E. M. Joad was still crying "hands off the Church of England; it's the only thing that saves us from Christianity," and it would have seemed incredible then that he would die in the bosom of the Establishment, declaring the village church and the village parson to be the salt savor of English life. If we picked up the American titles that found an export market, it was Winwood Reade's *The Martyrdom of Man,* and the glorious iconoclast H. L. Mencken hailing the Twilight of the Gods, and celebrating the demise of every romantic dream ("Love is the illusion that one woman is different from another"). Marx, Freud and the behaviorists laid their hard hands on the brittle fabric of our beliefs, and crumbled it. The church itself was temporizing with modernity and the scientific spirit, abandoning one inherited position after another, and those of us who retained minimum Christian standing ground—either from habit, timidity, or profundity—were hard put to it even to hold the right to discuss the issues of faith in a world in which the prevailing assumption was that, as a representative modern put it, "Christianity is dead, and the only question is, how to get rid of the body before it begins to smell too much." The same young modern was in a monastery at last report, which proves nothing except that the temper of the times has changed.

Dorothy Sayers has something to the effect that Christianity, once indicted as a soothing syrup for lowbrows, is now in danger of becoming a close preserve of the highbrows. She has in mind, no doubt, the erudite apologetics of Eliot and Fry,

Malraux and Merton, the vogue of Kierkegaard and Gerard Manley Hopkins. Certain it is, at any rate, that a member of the class of '57, sniffing the intellectual air of his time, would breathe, not necessarily a pious air, but an air more congenial to piety, than that which caught at our Christian lungs in 1929. The wheel has almost come full circle. *We* thought a thing was not true if it could not be proved: the contemporary axiom is that if a thing *can* be proved, it is bound to be trivial. Apart from the diverse piety of Joad deceased and the later Huxley, the more influential voices, if they do not make Christian affirmations, at least raise the issues of faith. Marxism has degenerated to Communism, behaviorism has given way to existentialism, which is a kind of secularized version of the word of Christ that the pure in heart shall see God. Just about the time that naturalistic presuppositions have been written into our college texts, every naturalistic presupposition has been called in question, and faith is on the boom. All this is not clear Christian gain, for an atmosphere congenial to piety is congenial to all kinds of piety, many of them spurious. But it does open new possibilities of Christian communication, and makes life that much more interesting.

Amos Wilder, in the Preface to his *Modern Poetry and the Christian Tradition,* puts the thing this way.

> The custody and future of the Christian tradition has to a considerable degree passed over into the keeping of non-ecclesiastical and even secular groups. The fateful issues of the Christian faith are often wrestled with more profoundly outside the church than within. . . .
>
> . . . In a period of cultural crisis like ours with its accompanying costs and anguish, the secular world has been constrained for its very life to identify the spiritual resources

needed for survival, and to come to terms in its own way with the moral and religious traditions of the West. It is not surprising, therefore, that the major works of contemporary literature are undeniably theological in character . . . on the margin of the biblical view of man and history.

This somewhat staid thesis Wilder develops very vividly in relation to modern poetry. We propose to roam a different area.

But before we pick our ground, one or two preliminary things ought to be said. It is arguable how far the new literary "orthodoxy" is the fruit of the chastening experience of totalitarianism, war and depression. There is a connection: that is clear enough. But while an age of crisis and anxiety has made some secular assumptions less immediately plausible, it is not clear that it has made them necessarily vulnerable. It all depends on what time scale the events are drawn on, and anyone who has an interest in maintaining an evolutionary and optimistic world view is free of course to hold it. And some who want to hold it indict the new orthodoxy as a sort of crisis-mentality. Especially in America, where life retains a spaciousness and openness almost unique in the world, there is a tendency to write the newer movements off as pathological, the fruit of excessive and abnormal pressures which breed neurosis. I'm not quite clear why men who have been caught in crisis are to be disqualified from interpreting it, but that in any event is the way the argument runs.

In an undergraduate class of mine we were studying an early book of Emil Brunner's,[1] *The Word and the World*, in

[1]Brunner, along with Karl Barth, was a spokesman of the so-called "crisis-theology" which developed an assault on theological liberalism and has since matured in the so-called "neo-orthodoxy," the most influential single theological movement in the contemporary church.

which he uses the phrase "above the abyss of perdition" as a description of the condition of modern man—or of any man. There developed in the classroom the kind of revolt with which the ordinary man—especially the American man—reacts to such an account of his condition. It is extraordinarily irritating to be told that we are more wretched than we feel—and the stark account of the human dilemma which the European moderns go in for is taken by the ordinary Joe Doakes, and the academic Joe College, to be a product of European psychopathology rather than a transcript of the facts of life. And it simply adds insult to injury to be exhorted to despair in German, and to feel that mysterious *Angst* (cosmic anxiety or whatever) which is the theme of the contemporary prophets of doom and gloom. For what the ordinary man derives from this is that he cannot get near to God unless and until life's sweet joys turn to dust and ashes; or at least until he can learn to call them dust and ashes, sit in the midst of them, and lament. Not, says he, for me.

I recall a debate on the matter between two British theologians which went something like this. Theologian A, a new convert to the "crisis" or "neo-orthodox" school, maintained with vehemence that God visits man for his redemption only when man confesses himself bankrupt, at the veritable end of his tether. The fullness of God can be joined only to our human emptiness. To this, Theologian B took the gravest exception. The redemptive moments, he said in effect, are our creative and joyous moments. A man is never more accessible to what the divine Charity has to give than in his times of exaltation: the high mutuality of married love, the crinkled and lovely face of a first-born. The debate was years ago, but

the issue is worth recalling. I would maintain that in the debate
thus far the point has been missed: the point that there is one
thing common to exaltation and desolation, namely, the end of
self-consciousness, hypocrisy and self-deceit. Both desolation
and exaltation can sweep the heart clean of obfuscating pride.
They are both close conjoined to humility. In experiences of
both types life is touched in its depths, below the protective
layers of pride and pretense. They engender that "purity of
heart" which Jesus said was the condition of knowledge of
God. Jesus, as Reinhold Niebuhr, the "neo-orthodox" theologian *par excellence,* is fond of pointing out, rebuked his con-
temporaries because they were capable of neither joy nor
sorrow, they neither danced nor mourned, they could plumb
life neither in its heights nor in its depths. And this is curious,
for the Jew characteristically is peculiarly endowed for both
joy and sorrow. The race breeds great tragedians and master
comedians. It may be that this is part of their "chosenness."
The Jew is, as Arthur Koestler says, "the exposed nerve of
humanity," and that not simply because of his historic vul-
nerability, but because of his unique human capacity. That is
one reason why we shall pay particular attention to his tradition.

Meanwhile I want simply to pick up the phrase "the exposed
nerve," and to take a look at Koestler himself and at two others
—not Jews as it happens—who seem to me to represent in our
day the articulate self-consciousness of a generation. They
are master interpreters of sorrow, and sorrow has been a massive ingredient of our life and of our time. But their work—
this is especially true of Graham Greene and Robert Penn

Warren—is not devoid of joy. The selection of these three is highly arbitrary. The simple fact is that I know them better than I do others—like Camus and Bernanos for example— who may be greater men or who may not. But these three speak to my condition, and I think to our common need. Arthur Koestler is a Hungarian Jew who, after work in the Communist Party, war in Spain and internment in France, has done most of his (anti-Communist) writing in England. I will let him speak out of Europe. Graham Greene is as English as they come, a literate convert to Roman Catholicism, gravely suspect by many of his coreligionists and therefore peculiarly interesting for our purpose. Robert Penn Warren is an established interpreter of American life both in prose and in verse. We deal only with his last poem. All three seem to me, even when they stop short of the Christian affirmation as do Koestler and Warren—and Greene too for his fictional purposes—to ask questions that scream for Christian answers.

EUROPE: *Arthur Koestler*

Koestler is in some ways the least interesting of our contemporary spokesmen because—on a prejudiced Christian view of the matter—he makes less use than do Greene and even Warren of the Christian categories of redemption and forgiveness. It would appear that for Koestler biblical and Christian faith simply does not offer a viable option—though he is fascinated by the Jew and by his own Jewishness, he is able only to describe and not to account for the distinctively Jewish stance of faith. Nonetheless he has pin-pointed, in his

symbolic figures of the *Yogi* and the *Commissar*,[2] the salient
options between which contemporary men—at least such contemporary men as live close up to the moral frontier—tend
to oscillate.

The *Commissar* is, of course, the symbol of revolutionary
logic and of revolutionary violence. If Communism is the contemporary form of natural religion, the Commissar is its prototype and exemplar. He deifies and conforms to the dynamics
of nature and history (which is by definition a part of nature,
with no real dimension of freedom in it). He submits not to
God, that superstitious projection of man's fears and longings,
but to nature's inherent and organic logic; and for the service
of God he substitutes a manipulative surgery wrought upon
the body of nature, and upon the bodies and souls of men,
which are by the same definition also part of nature.

So the commissar Ivanov in *Darkness at Noon,* in dialogue
with the old Revolutionary Rubashov, who has visited what
Ivanov calls "the metaphysical brothel" and come back dis-
eased with doubt about the validity of revolutionary logic and
its surgical procedures:

> There are [says Ivanov] only two conceptions of human
> ethics, and they are at opposite poles. One of them is Christian
> and humane, declares the individual to be sacrosanct, and
> asserts that the rules of arithmetic are not to be applied to
> human units. The other starts from the basic principles that a

[2]In his book of that title, *The Yogi and the Commissar,* he gives some systematic definition of the two terms. But the most dramatic account of the living
alternatives is in *Darkness at Noon,* possibly the greatest of his books. There are
related and illuminating discussions in *Arrival and Departure,* a study of the
psychology of a revolutionary, and in *Thieves in the Night,* an investigation of
the meaning of terroristic violence. His other books appear to me to be of less
importance.

collective aim justifies all means, and not only allows, but demands, that the individual be subordinated and sacrificed to the community—which may dispose of it as an experimentation rabbit or a sacrificial lamb. The first conception could be called anti-vivisection morality, the second, vivisection morality. Humbugs and dilettantes have always tried to mix the two conceptions; in practice, it is impossible. Whoever is burdened with power and responsibility finds out on the first occasion that he has to choose; and he is fatally driven to the second alternative.[3] Do you know, since the establishment of Christianity as a state religion, a single example of a state that really followed a Christian policy? You can't point one out. . . .

Rubashov's comment on this "vivisection morality" is: "To me it sometimes seems as though the experimenters had torn the skin off the victim and left it standing with bared tissues, muscles and nerves." "Well, and what of it?" said Ivanov happily: for presumably by every experiment some lesson in revolutionary manipulation has been learnt.

Rubashov cannot conform and takes his doubts to his death. But the question remains: What *is* the alternative to Ivanov's surgery? If sanity is not to be the simple conformity to the logic of historical nature, what is the option? And the option of course is the age-old alternative to natural religion, namely the rejection of nature and all its terrible dynamisms, and the cultivation of that *Yogi* withdrawal which begins in compassion for those who are caught in the ruthless clutch of existence, and ends in detachment from existence itself, with all its intolerable logic.[4]

[3]This was written, of course, before the "surgical operation" of the atomic bomb on Hiroshima. But the point since then is even more clear.

[4]Koestler's use of the *Yogi* symbol may not do total justice to Yoga, and it is certainly false to identify it with Christianity. But the symbol itself is clear and useful.

In the logical Communism of which Koestler's Commissar is symbol, history itself is deified, and conduct is determined as soon as the direction of the historical movement is determined. Life is to be lived purely and simply in the horizontal dimension of the cause-effect continuum of nature-history. There is no more sense in acting contrary to historic logic than there is in driving (as a British visitor is congenitally tempted to do) on the left-hand side on an American freeway. The only possible definition of the good cause is that it is the successful cause: the service of the lost cause, the forlorn and historically doomed cause, makes no historic sense, and is therefore "immoral" in the only meaning of that word for which there is room in thoroughgoing Marxism. The verdict of history is final, in the Hegelian sense that "the history of the world is the world's court of judgment." "History," as Hitler says (and this is one of the reasons for the curious affinity of Communist and Nazi, and their common detestation of the sentimental "liberals") "always forgives success." If the judgment of history is the last and final judgment, then all scruples are misplaced, and every ruthlessness is justified if it is justified in the historical event.

If we find the logic of this revolting, as Koestler's Rubashov does: if this God fails, the human option is the Yogi philosophy, the world-renouncing speculative or mystical thrust beyond and above the dire necessities of history. And this option has a mounting fascination for the Western intellectuals who a generation ago were under the spell of the Marxist *mystique*. Aldous Huxley's collation of the "perennial philosophy" is really a compendium of the world-renouncing strains in Greek philosophy and Asian spirituality. And this rhythm of attraction and repulsion is of the nature of the case. Natural religion is always passing into world-renouncing piety. For nature is both fascinating and revolting: man first looks *at* it and finds it fascinating; then finds it revolting and tried to look *through* it, to an undifferentiated realm in which the antinomies of nature are transcended. Hinduism for example has both strains: the idolatry of nature and its renunciation.

Koestler halts between these two opinions; Huxley states them in his *Grey Eminence,* and comes out strongly for the *Yogi* option. We shall argue later that biblical and Christian faith knows both options and rejects them both. But we stand indebted to Koestler for a penetrating statement of the human options as they pose themselves in the midst of the *social* struggle.

He has an illuminating reference at the end of his *Arrival and Departure* to the exhaustion of the *Yogi* and *Commissar* options and the need for a new "disclosure." It is not his latest writing but it sounds like his last word on the present question. The hero, Peter Slavek, a disillusioned Communist who almost took the other road but cannot resile from his unreasoning but irresistible impulse of justice, on his way into Europe on a "forlorn hope" mission against Fascism, writes thus to his mistress:

I'll tell you my belief, Odette. I think a new god is about to be born. That is the kind of thing one is only allowed to say at certain moments, but this is the moment, because in a few minutes I shall depart.

Praise to the unborn god, Odette. Don't try to divine his message or the form of his cult—this will be after our time. The mystics of today are as trite as the political reformers. . . .

I suppose that the Christian comment ought to be: "the un-born God, whom you ignorantly worship, we declare unto you. He is no new God, but the Ancient of Days, the God of Abraham, Isaac and Jacob, the God and Father of our Lord Jesus Christ, whose holy Son was slain neither as Yogi nor as Commissar, for He refused both roles." But how to make such a comment without impertinence and without arrogance?

GREAT BRITAIN: *Graham Greene*

Koestler pursues the human options in the sphere of social struggle and public duty, finding that they run out into nihil-ism or futility, that justice and compassion confound each other, that righteousness and peace never do kiss in this our life, and raises in the end a humanly unanswerable question.

Graham Greene is the master analyst of the personal life, of the intimacies of love and responsibility. He is an English con-vert to Roman Catholicism. The popular view tickets him as a Catholic novelist who writes enough successful thrillers—*It's a Battlefield, This Gun for Hire, Ministry of Fear, The Third Man*—to let him indulge his curious predilection for superstition and original sin, and even this he manages to make salable by spicing it with eroticism and by conforming to the prevailing and somewhat squalid preoccupation with the abnormal, especially the sexually abnormal. Slightly more reputably, he may be one of those odd and talented intel-lectuals who put on Catholicism as a somewhat exotic garment and cut something of a figure in Bohemia, their Catholicism being for the moment as live an option as Sartrean existen-tialism, and a good deal more live than Trotskyism. *Time* magazine began a fundamentally shrewd appraisal of Greene (October 29, 1951) with some such suggestion:

> It was one of those London cocktail parties where everyone showed up with a hangover. The host, a distinguished novelist named Graham Greene, roamed restlessly about his book-cluttered flat, listening to the mock-tragic tales of woe. Not to be outdone, the host confessed that he was feeling like hell: he had been up all night drinking with his priest.

For all I know Greene may indeed have spent one night or many drinking with his priest, but it would be a very great error to dismiss him as an anti-Puritan *poseur*. He is a great novelist, a great Catholic novelist, if indeed he *is* a Catholic novelist. This last is not mere Protestant priggishness: for he is under constant fire from the orthodox, and under threat of ecclesiastical censure in respect of at least one of his books, *The Heart of the Matter*, with its apparent justification of suicide. There is in fact a curious ambivalence in Greene. On the one hand he is like the adulteress-saint Sarah in *The End of the Affair*, who has caught belief as a sort of infatuation:

> I believe the whole bag of tricks; there's nothing I don't believe; they could sub-divide the Trinity into a dozen parts and I'd believe. They could dig up records that proved Christ had been invented by Pontius Pilate to get himself promoted, and I'd believe just the same. I've caught belief like a disease. I've fallen into belief like I fell into love. . . . I fought belief for longer than I fought love, but I haven't any fight left.

He will even, as in his defense of the Assumption proclamation, compound heresy to buttress dogma—witness his assertion that if Christ only be raised, then we have God resurrected and not man: Mary must ascend into heaven to take

humanity into the presence of God. A passionate conformity. . . .

And an equally passionate nonconformity, maybe born of
a belief that the Church always possesses a truth which is
larger than the Church knows, a faith that can be confined in
no dogma and in no rule. For instance, on Scobie's suicide in
The Heart of the Matter:

> [Father Rank]: "For goodness sake, Mrs Scobie, don't
> imagine you—or I—know a thing about God's mercy."
> "The Church says . . ."
> "I know the Church says. The Church knows all the rules.
> But it doesn't know what goes on in a single human heart."[5]

It is always an impertinence to fix on a man a label he would
disown: but even if I don't claim Greene for the Protestants, I
am free at least to accept his theological novels as a sustained
essay on the grace of God, the most powerful such essay in
modern literature, and to affirm that they do my Protestant
heart good.

There are four of them: *Brighton Rock, The Power and
the Glory* (published in America as *The Labyrinthine Ways*),
The Heart of the Matter and *The End of the Affair*. The critics
have made great play with the symbolic subtleties, but we shall
let ourselves be warned off them by Bendrix, the novelist in
The End of the Affair, who complains that the critics are
always finding subtleties in his novels of which he himself was
unaware. Green himself explains simply that *Brighton Rock*
is the story of a man who went to Hell, *The Power and the
Glory* the story of a man who went to Heaven, and *The Heart*

[5]It is worth remarking that there is hardly a possible criticism of Roman Catholic faith and practice that is not stated more lucidly and more persuasively in
Greene than in Paul Blanshard. Therein is the power of his apologetic.

of the Matter the story of a man who went to Purgatory. Since *The End of the Affair* is the story of a woman who went to Heaven, we may perhaps expect two more novels, one about a woman who went to Purgatory, and one about a woman who went to Hell . . . and what Greene, who knows female devilry, could do with this last!

There is not much of the grace of God in *Brighton Rock*. It is a terrifying picture of the meaning of unmitigated evil, of pride without pity. Pinky in *Brighton Rock* is Greene's witness to what is possible to man in the way of wickedness. Against him goodness is amiable and ineffectual, even laughable. Pinky is fascinated by evil, by the grisly splendor of open revolt against God, by the fearful freedom to choose Hell (John Donne's "dissolute liberty of eternal death"). He could be matched only by sanctity: mere human goodness is pallid in this lurid light. As one commentator says of all Greene's work:

> In his books normality appears to be romantic folly, a mere mathematical average, an unattainable equilibrium, a bourgeois deception, an affront to reality, a sentimental prejudice. . . . To Greene sanctity is abnormal, sin is normal. . . .

At first sight the title of *The Power and the Glory* is ironic. For it is the story of a failure. The "hero" (Greene's books actually *have* no heroes) is a priest who, from a mixture of priestly habit, inertia, and remnant courage, is caught by the revolution in Mexico and becomes part of the ecclesiastical underground. He is a miserable object: sodden in whisky, the father of a bastard by a village woman. Every good resolve is undone by his weakness. As he skulks among the villages, and is saved repeatedly from the soldiers at the cost of peasant lives, he reproaches himself continually that he has nothing to give his people. They deserve a saint and God gives them— what? The priest's own ludicrous self. He sticks at his priestly work first because he has no option, and second because of the strange conviction, born of his consecration, that even he and only he can "put God into people's mouths." He is caught at last and held to be shot. He plans a decent end, and in prison rehearses what he has heard of the sayings of the martyrs in the face of death. Maybe by a good end he can redeem a squalid life and a sullied priesthood: but his pious medita- tions are over the brandy bottle, and in the morning he has to be half-dragged, half-carried, to his death between two sol- diers. His death is as messy as his life: he is seen to make futile motions with his arms and to mutter something that sounds like "Excuse!" But no saintly last words, no ringing *"Viva el Cristo Rey!"* A drunken belch, a volley, and the end. The boy in the house near the square has been hearing his mother read about the martyrs:

> Reaching the wall, Juan turned and began to pray—not for himself, but for his enemies, for the squad of poor innocent Indian soldiers who faced him and even for the Chief of Police himself. He raised the crucifix at the end of his beads and prayed that God would forgive them. . . .
> "And that one," the boy said slowly, "whom they shot today. Was he a hero too?"

Not a hero, clearly, Greene appears to say, but a saint. (This is a novel, remember, about a man who went to heaven.) If salvation were any way yoked to achievement, this is damna- tion, for there is no achievement here. "If I had only one soul to offer, so that I could say, Look what I've done. . . ." No achievement, but most certainly the divine Charity. For where is grace more surely present than in the life whose tenor is "God be merciful to me, a sinner"? This is *The Power and the Glory* . . . of God and not of man.

Another theme of Greene's is suggested in *The Power and the Glory* and developed in *The Heart of the Matter*. In his last night the priest tries to make his confession without a confessor, but finds himself entangled in a mesh of self-pity, and of pity for the child he loves but could not acknowledge.

> "O God, help her. Damn me, I deserve it, but let her live for ever." This was the love he should have felt for every soul in the world: . . . For those were all in danger too. He prayed, "God help them," but in the moment of prayer he switched back to his child beside the rubbish-dump and he knew it was only for her that he prayed. Another failure.

My own salvation on the altar of compassion: is that the death of the self to which the self is called? Scobie in *The Heart of the Matter*, with a dependent wife and a mistress bound to him by a love which is half pity, kills himself lest his life make continuing mischief, yet is uncertain as he dies whether he dies to prevent their suffering, or to escape the misery of watching it. And suicide on his understanding of it is damnation:

> "One should look after one's own soul at whatever cost to another, and that is what I can't do . . ."

And since he must for his wife's sake make his death appear accident, he will compound his offense by taking the Host with her even after his suicide is determined upon.

> With open mouth (the time had come) he made one last attempt at prayer. "O God, I offer up my damnation to you.

Take it. Use it for them," and was aware of the pale papery
taste of his eternal sentence upon his tongue.

A man's first duty to save his own soul? No: a man's first
duty is to transcend his own self. Yet to detect that to lose the
life is to save it is to cry for grace, and for a succor from beyond the self. St. Paul's "I would I were accursed from Christ
for my brethren, my kinsmen according to the flesh": that is
the authentic Christian temper, a thrust beyond what is possible for man, a fire of compassion kindled by the divine
Charity. And so in *The End of the Affair:* "Let me forget me!"

The need for a virtue beyond human capacity, for a forgiveness which enables forgiveness, for a selflessness in which even
self-salvation is subordinated to the need of the other. There is
nowhere in modern literature—it may be in any literature—
such a prolegomenon to the Christian doctrine of grace.

THE UNITED STATES: *Robert Penn Warren*

Warren has written good novels which have made good
movies, but his latest book-length poem is dubious Hollywood
material. In *Brother to Dragons,* a lovely and a terrible poem,
he "resurrects" Thomas Jefferson to debate with him Jefferson's doctrine of man.

JEFFERSON:

If we might take man's hand, strike shackle, lead him forth
From his own monstrous nightmare—then his natural
    innocence
Would dance like sunlight over the delighted landscape.

And he would need no saint or angel then
To tread the monsters, for man's own free foot
Would tread them down like vintage in the press. . . .
That was only the old notion that propped my heart
    and thewed up
My human arm.

What changes Jefferson's mind, in Warren's account of it, is
an unspeakable deed out of his family's history, which Jefferson had kept hidden in the record, and hidden even from himself. As Warren tells it, the story is cruel almost beyond bearing, though the historic facts are firm, and fully documented.
Jefferson's nephew Lilburn, his sister Lucy's son, out of a perverted love for his dead mother turned in fury on his slaves,
and in the desolation of his heart sadistically slaughtered
George, a Negro boy whose only offense was that he loved
Lucy Lewis less than did her son. On the flimsiest pretext
Lilburn, with the enforced help of his brother Isham and in the
presence of the slaves, put George to death by inches, with a
meat ax on a chopping block in the meathouse of the estate.

Not only does "the scream in the midnight meat-house" shat-
ter Jefferson's "sweet lie . . . concocted out of nobleness"; it
forces a reassessment of what is in man:

JEFFERSON:

Oh, I'm not talking now about that boy
Hacked to his death, and his scream in the midnight
    meat-house.
For what's one nigger more in the economy of pain?

.   .   .   .

I am talking about the terrible texture in which
One episode of anguish evokes all anguish
And sets nerves screaming, and the white tendrils curl,
In black peripheries beyond the last stars.
I am talking about the circumstantial texture . . .

For the death of the boy George was not premeditated villainy,
but the product of a mesh of misshapen loves: Lucy's for Lilburn and his for her, with others entangled in a web of tender-
ness whose end-pattern is horror.

The human curse is simply to love and sometimes to love well,
But never well enough. It's simple as that.

And so, says Jefferson,

I have long since come to the firm and considered conclusion
That love, all love, all kinds, descriptions, and shapes,
Is but a mask to hide the brute face of fact,
And that fact is the immitigable ferocity of self.

.   .   .   .

There's no forgiveness for our being human.
It is the unexpugnable error. It is
. . . the one thing we have overlooked
In our outrageous dreams and cunningest contrivances.

And from this primal sin of being human there is no human
remedy. The guilt can neither be denied nor cured. There is
no use in saying "Lilburn is Lilburn . . ." and so "regard all
history as a private alibi factory,/And all God's gleaming
world as a ward for occupational therapy."

For if responsibility is not
The thing given but the thing to be achieved,
There is still no way out of the responsibility
Of trying to achieve responsibility.
So, like it or lump it, you are stuck.

. . . .

And whatever help we have is not by denial,
But in confronting the terror of our condition.
All else is a lie.

Jefferson tries hard to hold that, though knowledge is costly, "All is redeemed,/In knowledge," but from this position he is again thrown back:

Take George all huddled for the senseless axe,
The poor Laetitia,[6] who could never know
The truth she longed for, what her story meant.

This deep distemper is not healed by comprehension, but by a profounder therapy:

The recognition of complicity is the beginning of innocence.
The recognition of necessity is the beginning of freedom.
The recognition of the direction of fulfilment is the death of the
    self,
And the death of the self is the beginning of selfhood.

Koestler, Greene and Warren are at one in the perception that neither life nor history make rational sense, nor moral

[6]Laetitia in the poem is Lilburn's wife, the uncomprehending victim of his complex passions.

sense, nor any kind of sense, in and of themselves. There is an
incoherence, an inchoateness, in the very texture of things, and
every rational interpretation is an oversimplication. Either
this inchoateness is final, or else it can be transcended only
from a stance outside of self and history. The religious options
like the rational interpretations are oversimplifications: life
cannot be rejected, for it is burdened with meaning; it cannot
be accepted for itself and as it is, for it cannot articulate the
meaning with which it is burdened. In the sphere of social life,
according to Koestler, bare logic would give us either Commissar nihilism or Yogi world-renunciation. In the sphere of
the personal life, according to Greene and Warren, we are
called to a renunciation of self which to Warren is beyond the
capacity of the self, and which Greene hints is the stuff of
sanctity and the fruit of grace. We cannot realize our full
humanness, because we stumble continually over our
humanity. There is at least the suggestion here that the human
dilemma will need for its resolution not a resolve but a rescue.
"Oh that thou wouldst rend the heavens and come down. . . ."
"Oh sinful man that I am, who will deliver me from this body
of death?" But these are biblical words: it may therefore be
that in the biblical tradition the dilemma is at least understood.

Biblical religion . . . is not centered in the Absolute of metaphysical speculation any more than it is centered in the cycle of nature.

G. ERNEST WRIGHT *The Old Testament Against Its Environment*

2. *The Religion That Is No Religion*

The articulate self-consciousness of our generation begins to ask questions which scream for Christian answers. Yet the first comment out of the Christian complex of faith must be that the questions cannot be answered in the terms in which they are asked, nor can an answer be found among the available religious—which is to say human—options. For it is intrinsic to the Christian understanding of things that life and history do pose questions for which life and history do not provide the ingredients of a solution.

Koestler's *Yogi* and *Commissar* represent pretty adequately the available options: either the rejection of the world of nature and history with its intolerable ugliness and its unbearable antinomies, or the deification of nature and history, with the acceptance of its humanly intolerable logic. Even at this point it begins to be clear that if the questions are to be answered they must first be restated; and for our sordid Christian purposes we propose a restatement of the biblical account of the human and historical situation. And this ought not to be uncongenial: for Arthur Koestler, while he stands as yet uncommitted to the biblical categories or the authentic biblical loyalty, yet retains this at least from the inherited doctrine of Jewish "chosenness," that he takes the Jews to be "the exposed nerve of humanity," the articulate self-consciousness of every generation.

The doctrine of justification by grace through faith, which is the pervasive theme of this essay, implies a recognition of the emptiness of the human options, including the religious options. But if we are to come to the explicit doctrine of justification with some comprehension, we have to notice that it arises out of the very heart of the biblical world, is in fact spelt out between the covers of that most revered and most neglected of books, and cannot be discovered outside of the Hebrew-Christian scriptures and the tradition which stems from there.

The prime obstacle to the presentation of the Christian faith in our day is not an intransigent opposition to it. Now that Marxism has decayed into Communism the alternatives to Christianity are either flabby or uninviting. The problem is the genial assumption that we know what Christianity is, that we believe it after our fashion, and practice it within the limits of human capacity and contemporary opportunity. If we take a close look at this amiable notion, we can break it up a bit, and notice a number of forms of it which become explicit among the more articulate, for example among the undergraduates with whom I daily have to do.

The whole discussion on matters of faith is obfuscated by the uncritical assessment of *religion* which is presently current among the products of our American Christian—especially Protestant—nurture. The consensus is that religion is intrinsically a good thing, and that in its quintessence it consists in

belief in a Supreme Being and a moral law. The more sophisticated would talk about theism and ethical values, with the
latter more important and more certain than the former,
though they probably belong somehow together. This religion
of all good men, it is assumed, is to be found in every place
where men lift pious hands, and in many places where they
don't. It is common to all the great world religions, though consistently concealed under a crust of dogma, as it conspicuously
is in the Christian West. Being members of the American community we of course profess the local and indigenous variety
of it, which happens to be Christianity. This is on the whole a
harmless parochialism, though it does make us heirs of a great
deal of creedal and dogmatic lumber, and may harden into
"religious imperialism." Nevertheless, with a little added
sophistication, and some work on comparative religion, we can
quickly distinguish husk from kernel, and make our own the
common core of all religion, free from creedal encumbrance.

Understood in this fashion, religion is unqualifiedly a good
thing, and we ought to have more of it. Nothing would help
more towards world peace and unity than the coming together
of religious men, mature enough to surrender separatist
dogma, in a parliament of religions or something of the sort.

The thing is, of course, fantastic. It makes no human sense,
for multitudes of men who are united in their humanity are
divided in the sphere of faith. It makes no historic sense, for
religion is a highly dubious historic construct, as we shall see.
And it bears no resemblance at all to the standpoint of biblical
faith. In the world of the Bible, religion in this generic sense
is a very bad thing indeed, the prime and particular enemy of
authentic piety. In the New Testament Paul charges the

Athenians with being "too religious"; and it is not without
significance that one of the names for the Christians in the Hel-
lenic world was *atheoi,* atheists: for they would have none of
the available gods or the prevailing religions.

Religion is historically a very dubious construct. It is sometimes progressive, but as often reactionary; sometimes uniting,
sometimes divisive; it is sophisticated, and it is supersitious;
it is a nursery of charity, and a source of the most atrocious
cruelties. In many places and periods its effects are mischievous, even disastrous, by any humane and social criterion.
It has been argued by Norman Thomas only recently, for example, that contemporary India is a standing denial of the
pious thesis that the world can be saved by a revival of religion. For of the prevailing forms of piety India needs not
more, but less: the weight of piety on the masses of India is a
weight of oppression.

The conception of a basic unity between the great religions
is equally spurious and delusive. There is no real affinity between the world-renouncing piety of a thorough-going Buddhism and the earthy, materialistic faith of the Hebrews: nor,
in spite of Aldous Huxley, between the community-creating
creed of the Gospel and the individualism of the perennial
philosophy. The illusion of a coincidence in ideas could develop only out of plain misunderstanding; or when the authentic piety of Asia is influenced from the West; or when the
Hebrew-Christian affirmation of faith is emasculated and
spiritualized, as it congenitally is by this perverse and over-
pious generation. As a matter of fact there is more systematic
correspondence between Marxism and Christianity than there
is between Christianity and characteristic Asian spirituality.

Marxism as a Christian heresy bears the stamp of its origin. It knows that history has a meaning, even if it is mistaken about what that meaning is; it takes the material world seriously, though it goes on to take it too seriously and to forget that it "passeth away"; it knows something about collectivity even if it knows nothing of community. On all these points it stands in a perverse fashion closer to Christianity than, say, Buddhism does: for Buddhism cares nothing for history or for matter, and it can import a semblance of social concern only by the most blatant self-contradiction.[1]

Any satisfactory definition of religion must be noncommittal about its quality and its value. It is "Man's profoundest solicitude about the things he counts most valuable," as Ralph Barton Perry splendidly says. But that includes everything from Communism to the Navajo rain dance, as of course it should. The things man counts most valuable may not be valuable at all; and even if the things he counts valuable are really valuable, the "god" on whom he relies for them may or may not be able to deliver.

Another prevalent source of confusion is the popular notion of religion as functional; and for a rationalistic and moralistic generation this generally means that it is a source of rational truths and of ethical values. The fact is, as we shall

[1]"The illogical resolution which the Buddha formed at the moment of his enlightenment to preach the deep secret doctrine of salvation to all the world accounts for the fact that Buddhism grew out of a sublime mystical doctrine of redemption into a comprehensive world-religion with widespread congregations. But this transition led to a religious syncretism and therewith a transformation and degeneration of the original Nirvana mysticism of the Buddha." [Frederich Heiler. *Prayer (Das Gebet)*, Oxford, 1932.]

Heiler, I take it, talks of "degeneration" in terms of the original Nirvana impulse. For the moment we are not concerned with a judgment upon the element of commonalty in Buddhism, but simply to notice that it is in self-contradiction with its original genius.

see, that the Hebrew-Christian scriptures are singularly barren of general truths and of ethical principles. There is, for
example, no word in the Bible that can rightly be translated
"values." It is only a community far removed from the biblical
world which could imagine that the human problem is measurably eased when men know what is true and what is right:
even if what is true and what is right *could* be communicated
in abstract ways. For the Bible the human problem *begins*
when men know what is true and what is good; for the true
and the good meet him not as abstractions which illumine the
mind, but as implications of a divine self-disclosure which
lays a limitless and impossible demand upon the will.

One of the better of our Christian intellectual journals,
Motive, had a questionnaire a year or so ago which asked of
its student constituency a very symptomatic question: "What
do you expect to get out of religion?" The answers included
"peace of mind," "a coherent set of values," "personal inte-
gration," and all the rest of the functional desiderata. The
question which a biblical perspective might have suggested was
simply not put: namely, "How do I become the kind of person
who does not ask, 'What do I expect to get out of religion?'"

The truth is, as Edmund Wilson pointed out,[2] that to open
the Bible is to be introduced to "a whole point of view, a system of mental habits, which differs radically from those of the
West": and, he might have added, from those of the East. None
of our non-biblical categories will hold the biblical faith; most
of the characteristic biblical words are untranslatable. The
biblical faith is not even that "ethical monotheism" with which

[2] In *The New Yorker* for May 15, 1954, where he recounts his reaction to a reading of the Book of Genesis in Hebrew.

modern liberalism wants to equate it. If it's ethical monotheism we're after the Stoic is our man. Actually the Bible has
no ethics in the general philosophic sense; and as for monotheism, it knows of many gods though of only One who is "the
living and the true": and of this one only living and true God
it can use without embarrassment, as Martin Buber points out,[3]
a plural name.

This is probably enough to suggest that there is more in the
Bible than meets the casual modern eye. But the matter will be
clearer if we set out the biblical faith in its own distinctive
terms.

When Abraham moved out of Ur of the Chaldees, first with
his father to Haran, and then to the plains of Mamre in the
Land of Promise, there was a symbolic break with the religions of the world, and a new thing emerged in the midst of
the world and of men. For the religion of the ancient Near
East was of a type with all natural religion: it represented a
deification of the vitalities of the natural world, and the attempt to manipulate them by magic or to cajole them by
propitiatory sacrifice. For Abraham and his descendants all
such religion was idolatry, a source of confusion, illusion and
destruction. But the fascinating fact is that they broke from
it[4]—and rejected its later appeal in the form of Canaanitish

[3]In *The Prophetic Faith.* The name of course is *Elohim,* and the point need not
be pressed here, except to insist that the Hebrews always claimed to know more
of God's will than of his nature, and to be more concerned about obeying him
than defining him, even in consistent numerical symbols.

[4]"In Hebrew religion—and in Hebrew religion alone—the ancient bond between
man and nature was destroyed." [H. A. Frankfort. *The Intellectual Adventure of
Ancient Man* (Chicago, 1936) p. 342.] In his *Early Theological Writings* Hegel,

Baalism—without falling into the other human option, which is the rejection of the natural vitalities of the world as inimical and hurtful, and the attempt by contemplation or world-renouncing mysticism to reach an invulnerable stance beyond and above the changes and chances of the world. No doubt the cultural historian could argue that this second option was simply not available, at that time and in that place. But the historically momentous fact is that the Hebrews did not even move towards it, but developed instead a unique religious construct which involves neither the deification of the world nor its renunciation.[5] Whether Abraham be its historic originator, or a symbolic construct out of the faith of Moses and his successors, the fact is that the community of Israel as it emerges into clear historic sight is grounded in a conviction of faith which is derived neither from the empirical stuff of nature and general history, nor from speculation concerning a dimension of timeless truth unrelated to history.

As interpreted in the post-Mosaic tradition, what the Hebrews did was to focus on certain specific events within their own communal history, and to insist that these events— particularly the Exodus from Egypt and the Sinai-event of the giving of the Law—could be interpreted in only one way: namely, as the activity within history of a God of judgment and of mercy, of righteousness and love. His purpose for the

---

who is so often right about the fact and wrong in his judgment on the fact, rails at the Hebrews for precisely this breach of the primitive harmony of man with nature.

[5]"It is scarcely an accident that natural religion, when its course is not interrupted, works itself out into philosophy or mysticism. Biblical faith has always resisted complete surrender to either." [G. Ernest Wright. *The Old Testament Against Its Environment* (London, 1950), p. 75.]

whole world may be hidden, but he has a peculiar purpose for the people Israel, whom by these events he is calling to be his own people in the midst of the world, and to play a unique and crucial role.[6] The characteristic words for this divine dealing are *election* and *Covenant*. They are strongly personal and strongly corporate: they do not belong in the realm of speculation or of metaphysics.

The "psychology" of the communal commitment of faith is as mysterious as is any profound movement of the human spirit; but its meaning and effect is clear. It created a community which, as Herbert Schneider of Columbia says, "has no religion but only the Torah." This means, I take it, that the structure of faith and community which stems from here cannot be comprehended under any of the categories which the historian of culture might use to describe religion-in-general. One might have a stab at accounting for the phenomenon in terms of what Paul Tillich calls "a *Gestalt* of revelation." The conviction is born, not out of work on the empirical stuff of nature and history, nor out of reflection on the nature of Being, but out of the involvement of the community in a complex or configuration (*Gestalt*) of events which bear one compelling meaning and breed one irresistible conviction, a conviction henceforth invulnerable both to contrary evidence and to rational objection. This is all of the nature of personal encounter rather than of scientific work or philosophic speculation: and it is of course described by modern interpreters of

[6] His purpose for the whole world may be hidden, but it is clearly consistent with his righteous and loving will for Israel. "In thee shall all the nations of the earth be blessed." But Israel's calling is to play her proper role, not to fathom the whole design. Abraham Lincoln is in the true succession of his namesake the patriarch, when in his Second Inaugural he says, "The Almighty has his own purposes. . . ."

Hebraism like Martin Buber as having essentially the *I-Thou* character of personal confrontation.

This is the faith of the Covenant: a faith which creates a community and is nurtured in community. Hebrew faith is disparate in kind from natural religion, from rational religion, from mystical religion. God is to be found, to paraphrase Buber, not in the heart of hearts (by introspection), not in the holy of holies (by spirituality), not in the heaven of heavens (by mystical withdrawal): God is to be found *in the Community*. If he makes himself known in historic events which have the character of personal (Covenant) dealings, then he will be best known to those who take their loyal place in the community of his making and let him deal with them in the midst of the community.

This faith is profoundly historical, profoundly social. As such it has been the despair of the philosophers of religion, like Hegel, who scoff at the Hebrews' incapacity for reflection, which means in fact their inability to handle abstract and general concepts. The Hebrews may or may not have been incapable of philosophy: they were certainly uninterested in it. Their certainties were communal convictions, not rational conclusions. Their scriptures are barren of abstract definitions of God—or for that matter, of man. If God must be defined, then he is the One who brought Israel out of Egypt, made a people out of them and gave them his Law; who keeps covenant "to a thousand generations" (Deuteronomy 7:9). He has been faithful, that is to say, and will be faithful. If man is to be defined, then he is the one with whom God makes covenants, but who for his part congenitally breaks them.[7] If God

[7] The references to man as made "in the image of God" (Genesis 1:26), "a little lower than God" (Psalms 8:5), involve not metaphysical distinctions, but this capacity for covenant-making, covenant-keeping and covenant-breaking.

is to be systematically distinguished from man and man from the animals, then it is in some such way as this that the Hebrews would go about the matter. They would say that the animals don't make covenants, man makes them and breaks them, God makes them and never breaks them. This may infuriate the philosopher who wants to discriminate between biological and rational nature and so on, but it has its own homely validity, and a certain precision.

The anthropomorphism of the Hebrew scriptures, which is so disturbing to the more delicate-minded, is no more than a determination to keep all thought of God, and all talk about God, on this personal level, and to use neither subpersonal symbols nor abstract notions. Hebrew faith will not place God among the particularities of existence, which are accessible to observation; but equally it refuses to speak of God in universals or generalities, which are the fruit of speculation. It will worship neither the idols fashioned of wood and stone, nor the idols fashioned of reflection, which it calls frankly "imagination." For Hebrew faith the personal symbol is inevitable because it is only the person—as distinct from the thing or the concept—who can be identified yet never known, or who can in another sense be known yet never exhausted and so never defined. It is only the person who is more illimitably mysterious the better he is known. So the Hebrews have God sitting upon the circle of the earth, seeing, hearing, smelling (and finding the odor of hypocrisy peculiarly offensive), repenting, working, resting—and then, unable to rest, "rising up early" to send his prophets and continue his holy controversy with his people: all this with a brash and hearty disregard of the philosophic proprieties, but with an equally

hearty, positive and salutary avoidance of the idolatry either
of the thing or of the concept.

This God is verily a God who hideth himself (*Deus ab-
sconditus* as the theologians have it). He is known somewhat
as a person is known: that is, when he gives himself to *be*
known, in his acts, his words, his self-disclosure and self-com-
munication. But behind and beyond all that is known of him
in act and word is unfathomable mystery: his ways are higher
than our ways, his thoughts than our thoughts, even as the
heaven is above the earth. In the mystery of his self-giving he
has a way of by-passing the expectation of all reasonable men,
just as love does in its mysterious movement. He hides himself from the wise and discloses himself to the simple. He in-
habiteth eternity, yet he is known not to those who probe
eternity's secrets, but to the humble and the contrite in heart.
His ways are past finding out. There is no stance from which
a reasonable man may demand that God behave like a reasonable man. Israel itself is away ahead of the modern sophisticate who protests that God should disclose himself in timeless truths and general concepts, and not, absurdly, in the
trivial history of an obscure and unphilosophically-minded
race of peasants.

> *How odd*
> *Of God*
> *To choose*
> *The Jews.*

But it was the Jews who said it first. The "mystery of Israel"
was a mystery first *for* Israel. "God did not set his love upon
you, nor choose you, because ye were more in number than

any people: for ye were the fewest. . . ." (Deuteronomy 7:7).
The compulsion of belief which came upon Israel was a
strange compulsion, an embarrassing compulsion. The complex of events which made their history, and which could be
read in no other way than as the pressure of the divine love[8]
and the demand of the divine righteousness, were not events of
their choosing. The calling of Israel is the prime mystery of
grace. It is in some such context of faith as this that Abraham
and his successors discovered how to avoid both world-
renunciation and unqualified world-acceptance. They found
or were given a solution to the perennial human problem;
which is, as G. K. Chesterton put it, to love the world without
being at home in it. They built cities, which a world-renouncing piety does not, but they did not kid themselves—at least
when they attended to what the prophets told them they did
not—that they were continuing cities. They bred neither Yogis
nor Commissars. And from this stance of faith they spelt out
their own version of truth and of goodness, of man and of history, of sin and of redemption, which is the necessary prolegomenon to the Christian understanding of life.

On the Hebrew view of the matter, truth-for-life (existential
truth if we use the contemporary jargon) is the fruit neither
of observation nor of speculation. They did not claim that the
empirical stuff of life made sense in and of itself, and so they
were not taken aback by the inimical or contradictory facts of
life and history; nor did they claim that the free and autono-
mous reason could impose rationality upon life's intractable
disorder. Nothing could have been more alien to the Hebrew

---

[8]*chesed:* which is translated in most of our Bibles as loving-kindness, but is
actually again untranslatable except in the context of Covenant-love and Cove-
nant-loyalty.

mind than the nonsense about "proofs for the existence of God." In view of what they knew of God's ways and his will from his dealings with the fathers and with them, it would be patently gratuitous to talk about proving him (in the sense at least of rational demonstration of his existence). Truth for them was given in the particular event which tradition calls *Sinai:* or rather it was given in the complex of events which had its initiation and interpretation at Sinai. This is the revelatory *Gestalt,* which lays upon the man who is enmeshed in it a compulsion of belief which is susceptible neither of rational nor experimental vindication or refutation. What was true for the Hebrews was not what was rationally or experimentally true, but what was involved in the revelatory and community-creating Event, which is to say in the divine encounter, the Covenant. The issue thenceforward is not theism or atheism, but *idolatry:* either the one only living and true God, who makes himself known *there,* or the gods of the nations, which are idols.

This determines, for example, the prophetic consciousness and the character of prophetic authority. There are certainly ecstatic elements mixed up with the prophetic history: but when Amos or Isaiah lay upon the people the demands of justice with their shattering "Thus saith the Lord. . . ." they are appealing not to a private and interior revelation, but to a public revelation and an acknowledged obligation. The accent is not "God told me, and I tell you . . ." but rather "You know as well as I do . . ." what the Covenant requires. And before we write this off as primitivism and irrationalism, we ought to notice that it has its analogy in the way in which all our life-forming decisions and commitments are in fact shaped. For our own basic loyalties—to truth, for example, or to freedom —we would be hard put to it to find rational or experimental validation. That truth is worth cherishing, that freedom is worth dying for: these affirmations of faith are the result less of speculation and experimentation than of community nurture and personal encounter. They are bred in us, rather than imposed upon us by the compulsion of fact or of reason.

And as with truth, so with goodness. What was *right* for Israel was not "rational standards rationally perceived" (which is one version of natural law) nor what was required for an harmonious relation to the natural world (another version of natural law) but what the Covenant required, which might at times be both irrational and unnatural. The Hebrew Scriptures are as bare of philosophic ethics as they are of philosophic theism.

The content of this Covenant faith, which is historical and social rather than rational or experimental, has the most positive meaning for man's understanding of himself and his world.

The created world is good, for since it is the Covenant God who made it, and who takes delight in it, there can be no approach to God by withdrawal *from* the world, and no service of God save a righteous life *in* the world. "God created the heavens *and the earth* . . ." so that there is here no dualism of spiritual and material, as if the former were hallowed and the latter nasty and poor. Biblical "spirituality" is not the renunciation of the material, but its proper and godly use. The world of things and the life of men, all the natural vitalities

of the world, are not only justified by their creation, but sanctified by the Creator's delight in them. "God saw everything that
he had made, and behold, it was very good." And from this
benediction nothing is excluded, not even, as some perversely
imagine, the life of sex. For before this benediction is spoken
Adam and Eve are made male and female and blessed as such
and exhorted "Be fruitful, and multiply. . . ." The primeval
account of Adam and Eve in the plenitude of created and
creative power, inhabiting "a garden filled with all manner of
fruits," is a picture of such divine exhilaration in creation as
forces us, if we are asked to say summarily why God made the
world, to affirm that he made it for fun! There is no purpose
in it save the purpose of joy: the joy of the Maker in the world
of his making, and the derivative and reciprocal joy of the
world in the world itself and in him who made it. It is from
here that there stems the characteristic Hebrew attitude to the
world of things, which has no faintest touch of world-renouncing spirituality about it. It is rather a lip-smacking, exuberant
delight in the ingenious beauty and variety of the created
world; in wine and milk, oil-olive and honey. It is a world
whose paths drop fatness, where the little hills rejoice on every
side. Such a world has a place for heroism, but none for
asceticism. Asceticism in Hebraism is always an aberration.

Man is a creature of unimaginable dignity. He is made out
of the earth, the good earth: "God formed man out of the dust
of the ground . . . ," and this good earth is enkindled with
the divine life . . . , "and breathed into his nostrils the breath
of life, and man became a living soul (*nephesh*)." There is a
mystery here, even in the text: for the word *nephesh*, which is
ordinarily translated "soul," is in fact virtually untranslat-

able, as are so many of the crucial Hebrew words. It is not "soul" simply in the sense of a life-principle, for the animals have that; nor is the divine life to be equated with the light of reason, since the God of the Hebrews is emphatically not a rational principle. "Personality" has too many modern overtones, so that won't do. The clue again is in the notion of the Covenant. It is the character of God to enter into Covenant with man, in righteousness and love. The man, then, to whom God gives his *nephesh*, who is made in God's image, becomes the kind of creature who has the capacity for covenant-making, for reciprocity. He is made for the kind of society which can be constituted only out of freedom. What is at stake in all this is not that man has some special talent or capacity as compared with the rest of the created world—though he does have that: what is at stake is that man is elected to a special status and a special responsibility. He is made "a little lower than God," as Psalm 8:5 should actually read; yet by the character of his created being he is bound both to God and to the world, in personal responsibility to the former and in personal authority over the latter. He is given, as the record says, "dominion over the earth"; he is under God and over the world. Here again the *motif* is joy: for in so far and for as long as man retains his true and given status, he has the tranquillity of proper order, the "joy of the Lord," the enjoyment of the garden-world and all its fruits.

It is of course not necessary to say that this is mythology and not history. It is authentic myth, the transcript of the Hebrew consciousness as it spells out the meaning of life on the basis of the revelatory events which determined the Covenant-character of the community, and all its thoughts of God.

What we have here is a delineation of what original righteousness means: and since righteousness is simply *rightness,* the
content of the story is God's primal intention for the children
of men. In another characteristic Hebrew idiom, this is what
holiness (wholeness) means: it depicts how well everything is
ordered when God orders everything. And to this affirmation
of a God who in loving-kindness desires for man nothing but
fullness of joy, the Hebrew will cling though the whole world
shout a denial, and the race be bound in affliction and iron:
for he conceives this faith to be authenticated not in reason
and not in observation, but in the witness of the fathers to
God's faithful dealing with them, and his own strange dis-
covery that in the same faith he can go through the valley of
the shadow of death and yet fear no evil.

Sin is terrible and redemption is costly. This view of man
implicitly excludes a number of common and current versions
of the human dilemma. It denies, for example, that version of
the human problem, so characteristic of Asian spirituality and
now seducing many a hard-pressed occidental sophisticate,
that existence itself is the evil, and that salvation is by way of
negation of self and world, and the reabsorption of the ego in
some kind of undifferentiated Being. Of such a view there is
no trace in Hebrew thought, at least in the main line of the
scriptural witness. It denies and rejects also all rationalistic
and naturalistic solutions of the human problem. The former
would locate the human essence and therefore the human problem in the reason. It would find the cause of our affliction in
ignorance, and would expect it to be dispelled by sophistication, by education, by pedagogy; or else, from the same starting point, it would assume that the problem of reason is its

corruption by nature, its frustration by the intractable stuff of the subrational world of things and of desire. But here again the problem is one of maturing the reason, by time and by experience. This view runs out into the modern scientific world view, in which nature is to be progressively mastered and subjugated to technological reason, whose preliminary triumphs have already dispersed many of the ghosts conjured up by an obscurantist piety, and promise ever-increasing ascendancy over the forces which are inimical to man's life. It sounds great; until we notice that men now fear the scientists more than they feared the ghosts. Which would be no surprise to men who allowed themselves to be tutored by biblical faith, which breeds no illusion that reason riding the historic tide has the sure mastery of the future. For in biblical faith nature, reason and history are all perverted by a most radical distortion, which is to be identified neither with the down-drag of the flesh, with rational inadequacy, or with historic immaturity. Just as man's primal dignity consists not in any natural or rational faculty, but in the Covenant-status into which God invites man, on the basis of his given freedom, so his wretchedness derives not from ignorance—in the biblical record the sorry story of man's distress begins with man's acquisition of knowledge; nor from sensuality—for it is the divine hand that clothes man about with flesh: it originates in the dimension of freedom, in the rebellion of the self in the interests of the self. Man is no longer content to be, as in his authentic status he is, under God and over the world. He distorts the true order of things by grasping at autonomy, in a self-idolatry which not only throws his whole perspective out, but makes his actual life a self-contradiction and a lie. This is "total depravity" indeed; not in the sense that man is henceforth incapable of heroism or compassion (the Bible says man is a sinner, not that he is a scoundrel), but in the sense that his prideful self-assertion touches with corruption every motion of his being, turning the speculative reason into an ideological instrument (Marx), turning sex into lust (Freud), making technological reason a source of mounting fear. It makes no sense to suggest that such a profound self-alienation of the self will be healed by pedagogy or by progress. This is tetanus-death, in which the self turns in upon the self, and so makes impossible those free and fruitful relations with God and the neighbor for which it is born. It can be freed from the deathly circle only by the injection of some serum which can set the process of life to rights again.

In personal terms more congenial to the biblical idiom, man can get back his primal dignity only by giving up his rebellion, and this the natural man is incapable of doing. The egocentricity which perverts all reason cannot be mastered by an appeal to reason, nor can the deliverance of the self from itself come from that will which is intrinsically self-will. There is no stance in the human psyche from which an attack can be leveled against this radical distemper, since the distemper poisons the whole self. Man spells out his life-history on the basis of an assertion—a self-assertion—which is itself a lie, and so makes tragic nonsense of the whole.

The Bible is wiser than Kant in recognizing that man *is* commanded what he cannot perform, which is the surrender of the self; and in recognizing that history, which is the history of man's rebellious freedom in its conjunction with nature, poses problems for which it does not provide the ingredients of a solution.

The human dilemma, according to the biblical faith, is such that it calls not for a resolve but for a rescue. Since man's nature is defined by his relationship to God, the perversion of his nature is a breach of that relationship which takes two for its healing. That is why the Bible talks not of sophistication— of wisdom in the classic sense—but of grace and repentance. And that is why, when the Bible approaches the problem of history, it talks not of progress but of the coming of a Messiah. For the perversion of the self is the perversion of history, so that every rational and historical advance introduces new possibilities of the prideful perversion of life. On this view history is not a problem-solving process but itself part of the problem. It cannot be without meaning, since it has its origin in God: it cannot have its meaning in itself, since it is compound of evil. Human nature and history cry for a fulfillment which must take the form of renovation or redemption, and such renovation can come only from divine intervention. This is the root of Hebrew Messianism: the conviction that history has a meaning and will have a fulfillment, but neither can be woven on the loom of history itself.

Batter my heart, three-person'd God; for, you
As yet but knock, breathe, shine and seek to mend;
That I may rise, and stand, o'erthrow me, and bend
Your force, to make, blow, burn and make me new.
I, like an usurp'd town, to another due,
Labour to admit you, but Oh, to no end,
Reason your viceroy in me, me should defend,
But is captiv'd, and proves weak or untrue.
Yet dearly I love you, and would be loved fain,
But am betroth'd unto your enemy:
Divorce me, untie, or break that knot again,
Take me to you, imprison me, for I
Except you enthrall me, never shall be free,
Nor ever chaste, except you ravish me.

JOHN DONNE *Holy Sonnets* XIV

3. A Religion to End All Religion

There are certain aspects of Hebrew faith which are best looked at as they inform the New Testament and shape the life and faith of the Christian Church. For it is clear that the primitive Christian affirmation, the formative and normative testimony which is writ large in her scripture, creeds and hymns, is that that which is promised has come about, that He who was promised has come "in the flesh," that the events which were associated with the life and death of Jesus of Nazareth matched and outmatched what God had done for His people in the Exodus and at Sinai. The cry of Israel, "Oh that thou wouldst rend the heavens, and come down . . . ," is an-

swered by the opening announcement of the New Testament,
"Blessed be the Lord God of Israel, for he hath visited and
redeemed his people." The events which brought the Church
into being, said the Christians, were as crucial for life and
history as were the Exodus and Sinai in their time, as crucial
even as the creation of the world itself, since by them was
initiated a new man, a new community, a new creation. How
had this new thing come about?

The burden of the Hebrew faith is that the meaning of history is hidden, and what is known is simply the calling to
which Israel is called. Abraham, "the father of all the faithful," went out not knowing whither he went, and his loving
obedience to the enigmatic "call" is a paradigm of Israel's
essential business in the midst of the world. She is called to
a venture in holiness, in the Hebrew understanding of it, which
is another word for obedience. The unraveling of the historical
riddle, the cure of the human and social distemper, the lifting
of the weight of sin and death, the fulfillment of life's hidden
but joyous meaning, are in some way dependent on the faithfulness of the people of God. Both Law—a transcript of the will
of God—and Cult—a ceremonial of dedication—bear witness
to this conviction that the issues of life and death for the communities of men depend upon Israel's diligent performance
of her Covenant obligation. The rationale of this is not easy to
recover. It depends for one thing upon a powerful consciousness of solidarity which it is difficult for us congenital indi-
vidualists to understand. Both sin and righteousness were
taken to be contagious. For example Achan's sin (Joshua 7)
involved the destruction by fire of his whole house, lest from
this point of contagion the whole community be infected with

evil: and in some such sense it was also believed that there
was a contagion of holiness, so that the performance of righteousness by the nation, or by a group within it (the holy
Remnant) or by one man, would inject health into the afflicted
body of mankind. The tradition includes some odd illustrations of this essential conviction; for example the notion that
if the Sabbath could be kept just once, perfectly, the Day of
the Lord would dawn; or the idea that if not the whole nation,
but just fifty-one per cent of it, would keep the Law . . .

It would appear that in the early centuries of Israel's history this profound conception of the Covenant calling, of the
vocation of holiness, was applied to the whole nation. It is not
because the prophetic spokesmen are pacifists that they rebuke
the people for attempting their security by military maneuver:
it is because they believe Israel's weakness to be providential.
It is nonsense for Israel (or for Judah), say the prophets in
effect, to try to play the game of power politics. Their weakness makes it impossible. Their business is to notice that God
has called them in their weakness—"the least among all
people"—to a unique work among the nations. Their special
and particular business is to show the world what God can do
with an insignificant people who perforce and from faith puts
its sole trust in Him, and stakes everything, not on might nor
on power, but on meticulous holiness and the power of God's
Spirit.

When the northern kingdom was destroyed by the Assyrians
in 722 B.C. the moral was obvious. They had fallen by the
weight of their own political cleverness (aggravated by overt
disobedience) and the onus now fell on Judah and Jerusalem.
But again, as Jeremiah says, the fatal thing would be to sub-

stitute idols, even the idolatrous faith in the survival of the
nation itself, for the one only living and true God. That is the
sure way to "make this house like Shiloh," to bring destruction
upon the South as it had come on the North. But even if the
Holy City itself should fall, God remaineth faithful, and he
will honor the witness of a holy core within the nation, the
Remnant. In historic fact no such Remnant appears, and there
appears to be a connection between the failure of this hope
and the development of the idea of a personal Messiah, the
conception that upon one man, a king it may be, or a man out
of the people, conspicuous for his costly devotion to the cause
of God and the people, will fall the redemptive role. There is
a suggestion in the Book of Daniel that before the Old Testament period ended, the hope of salutary holiness coming out
of the stuff of mankind had failed too, and the "Son of Man"
figure in Daniel and in later writings may represent the conviction that if such a deliverer is to come God will have to
send him, since human nature has shown itself incapable of
generating redemptive holiness and the perfection of obedience. Be that as it may, the focus in all these symbolic figures
is upon obedience. For example, the Hebrews knew human
nature well enough not to indulge the type of expectation
represented by Plato's philosopher-king. They knew that you
cannot join power to wisdom without corrupting the wisdom:
and the king who becomes the type of Messiah is not Solomon
who was proverbial for wisdom, but David, who was conspicuous neither for wisdom nor, curiously, for virtue, but
who did know what the Covenant meant, and was mindful of
it even in his recurrent disobedience.

The condition of redemption is still Covenant-obedience, so

that if the Messiah does come as king he will be in the succession of David, the apotheosis of the righteousness which David partially embodied. For only the perfection of obedience can join earth to heaven again, open again the gates of Eden, make the lion to lie down with the lamb, make righteousness and peace to kiss. If the "man from heaven" figure who appears in the latest writings does represent the abandonment of the hope of a Messiah out of the body of mankind, then the sequence of the thought is complete. The ambiguities of history are seen to be beyond human resolution, yet if God be faithful they must one day be resolved: hence the Messianic thrust beyond human possibilities to a divine *deed*. It is this divine deed which according to the initial Christian proclamation has been accomplished in Jesus as the *Christ* (which word is simply the Greek form of *Messiah:* the One whom God sends).

The New Testament lovingly and diligently assembles the symbolic forms of the Old Testament expectation, and refers them all to Christ. He is the fulfillment of the Law: by the perfection of his obedience he testifies both to the Law's validity as representing the divine claim, and to its inadequacy as a mechanism of salvation. He is the sacrifice to end all sacrifices (especially but not only in the Letter to the Hebrews): by the perfection of his self-offering he validates all that the Cult proclaimed of the sanctification of life and of atonement for sin, and makes any further cultic offering redundant. He is the King of the Jews, of the lineage of David: but as King he mysteriously joins power to wisdom, by transmuting power into triumphant meekness, and wisdom into love. He is the suffering Servant of the Lord; and from the Christian point of view it matters not at all whether the writer of Isaiah 53 in his talk of the Servant, "he was numbered with the transgressors, and he bare the sin of many," had in mind the nation, a remnant within the nation, or one man bearing the sins of many men. Whatever he meant and more than he meant is realized in Jesus Christ, who in yielding up his life unto death is the one-man Israel, the one-man Remnant, the Covenant-man who undertakes in his own single body the venture of obedience to which Israel had from time immemorial been called. To this most notable obedience God responds by breaking for His sake the power of mankind's ancient enemies, by lifting the weight of guilt and destroying the power of death: a new and living way is opened into the presence of God, man gets back his primal dignity by giving up, in Christ and for His sake, his perennial rebellion, and the New Covenant of Jeremiah's expectation comes into being.

This is the minimum Christian proclamation, in which promise is matched by fulfillment, and the Old Testament witness comes to its crown and climax. It is intelligible only if we take seriously the Hebrew notion of covenant solidarity, and accept it that the contagion of holiness is as real and powerful as the contagion of evil. In that sense it can be true that Christ sanctified himself for the sake of all. The New Testament phrase "in Christ" does not have a mystical reference: it refers not to mystical absorption but to the solidarity of community.

This is the minimum Christian proclamation, in the barest biblical terms. But Christian reflection has discovered other than this and more than this—more, that is to say, than was prefigured in the prophetic expectation.

Let us try to put it in such terms as make connection with

the articulate self-consciousness of our generation as we have seen it partly spelt out. And since we cannot trace every strand of the biblical thought, we shall attend particularly to what is involved in the notion of Christ as *fulfiller of the Law.*

In the first place *He states the Law perfectly.* There has been considerable discussion among Jewish and Christian scholars, and between Jewish and Christian scholars, as to whether there is or is not anything unique or original in "the ethical teaching of Jesus." Those who want to construe Christianity as an elevated morality are bound to maintain that there is; but there has been a progressive accumulation of Old Testament and rabbinic parallels for most at least of the sayings of Jesus. From the point of view which is here maintained the question is misconceived. It is possible to argue that Jesus did increase the range and depth of the demand of the divine Law, and that explicitly, but nothing essential depends on this. The "new wine" of the new Covenant is still wine, the new Commandment is still a commandment. The recorded teaching of Jesus in matters of conduct is fragmentary, simply because he took the *corpus* of the biblical law for granted, and invited inquirers to remember what they had been taught in the rabbinic schools. What he does do, whatever more he does, is to make luminous what had before been opaque. The Sermon on the Mount, with its delineation of an utterly disinterested love, is the apotheosis, the quintessence, of the divine Law. The Law had always been conceived to be in some sense a transcription of the divine will: it now becomes clear that what was adumbrated in the older forms of the Law, when fully disclosed and articulated is a life utterly cleared of isolating egoism, and established upon the selfless love of God and the neighbor.

"Thou shalt love thy neighbor as thyself" (Matthew 19:19) is not, as the popular exegesis has it, an exhortation to elevate the neighbor to parity in love with oneself: it is an exhortation to transfer to the neighbor the love which the "natural man" lavishes upon himself.[1] There is of course a paradox here, and the very word "love-commandment" is a contradiction in terms. In his *Early Theological Writings* Hegel made great play with this, suggesting that Jesus is seeking only to make explicit what is natural to man, and it is the limitations of a language dominated by legalism which make it necessary for him to speak of a "commandment." But the point is in the paradox. If the will of God is the ultimate constitution of man's being, and if that constitution is a spontaneous selflessness, and if this when he hears it has the form of an external command, it means that man's being is distorted, corrupted, dirempted. So that when the ethical demand is stated in its final rigor, as it is in the Sermon, it raises the question of redemption, of renovation, of the transformation or reconstitution of man's very self. "Be ye transformed," says St. Paul, "by the renewing of your mind" (which is to say, your life), "that ye may know what is that good, and acceptable, and perfect will of God." The implications of all this are most perfectly developed in the teaching of Martin Luther, to which we return. But meanwhile we should notice what more is involved in the conception of Christ as fulfiller of the Law.

In the second place, not only does Jesus as the Christ state

[1] Cf. Luther, *Romerbrief* ii, p. 337f. "Therefore I believe that by this precept 'as thyself' man is not bidden to love himself, but the vicious love is exposed wherewith he loves himself in fact; that is to say, thou art wholly bent upon thyself and turned to love of thyself (curvus es totus in te et versus in tui amorem), from which thou shalt not be made straight, except thou entirely cease to love thyself and, forgetful of thyself, love thy neighbour alone."

the Law in its quintessence as the love-commandment, but He, as the one-man Israel, perfectly performs it. With transparent devotion to the will of God and the good of the people he makes a perfect oblation of Himself, counting not his life dear.

And *in the third place*, He fulfills the Law in forgiveness, by perfect comprehension of the human dilemma in the face of a humanly impossible demand, by ensconcing in his love the sinful children of men, dying for them while they are yet sinners.

Let me attempt an illustration of what is involved here. In a parish where I was minister there was a well-marked group of alcoholics, who drank whisky when they could get it and methylated spirits when they could not, derelicts whose very body tissue craved the drug. After a bout they would turn up at the house, sleep it off in a room held for the purpose, and wake to a sobbing recognition of the plight they were in, their incapacity to meet their most elementary obligations, their dark diremption from the community of freedom and responsibility. At that point I could have failed them in one of two ways: if I had tried to stem their tears with the suggestion that they stop torturing themselves with an impossible standard, I should have betrayed them, for their remnant manhood was *in* their tears. On the other hand, I could have failed them by abandoning them: for in the recognition that they were loved in their helplessness there was at least some reassurance and some resource. I don't know that I succeeded, but I do know what was involved. And somewhere there is a poor refraction of what the Gospel means: that Christ not only calls us to perfection by His word and example, but companies with us this side of our perfection.

Paul the Apostle, especially in the Roman and Galatian Letters, gives this insight its normative Christian expression. The Law as it magnifies the righteousness of God in the religious consciousness of the devout Hebrew, articulates itself finally as an illimitable and impossible demand; it summons man to be what he is and yet is not—spontaneously aligned with and devoted to the divine will in the Covenant. Such is man's nature, but such is not man's potentiality as man. Moral maturity and moral despair are here conjoined. The claim that the divine will is even measurably within human reach, that the abyss between our achievement and the demand of holiness is passable from the human side, is the sign not of moral maturity, but of moral idiocy. "O wretched man that I am, who shall deliver me from this body of death." At this point the "new Law" of love is not a source of reassurance but of desolation. The Law of love which by its nature must be written on the heart is by its nature more demanding even than "the law of commandments contained in ordinances." This Luther for example knew well:

> . . . this understanding of the law spiritually is far more deadly, since it makes the law impossible to fulfil and thereby brings man to despair of his own strength and abases him, for no one is without anger, no one without lust: such are we from birth. But what will a man do, whither will he go, when oppressed by such an impossible law?

As Anders Nygren says in commenting on this Luther passage:

> The more seriously he [Luther] takes the commandment to love God with all his heart, and the more strict the demand that the love of God shall be pure and unselfish, the more impossible it becomes. It is not merely an external legalism of which

Luther perceives the inner impossibility, but he has in view the highest and deepest of all commandments, and the most inward of them, the Law of Love. . . . External commandments are easier to deal with, but the commandment which requires love with all the heart can only be a law which damns. In the monastery Luther learnt by personal experience that the Commandment of Love in its most intense and inward form is the most tyrannical law; indeed, it is a real devil for the troubled conscience.[2]

Join the impossibility of the love-commandment to the paradox in the very notion of a commandment to love, and the question of redemption, of renovation, becomes inevitable: How do I become the kind of person who *can* love, and who can love *without* command?

Again we come to the point where the human dilemma is such that it requires not a resolve but a rescue. "The death of the self is the beginning of selfhood": the self must be delivered from the self.

It is this dilemma which is compassed in the Christian economy of salvation. We shall set out Luther's version of it, which is not only most influential in the formation of classical Protestantism, but in our judgment the most clear and consistent expression of the primitive Christian affirmation which the great tradition provides.

In the first place the problem, according to Luther, is totally misconceived when it is stated in "religious" terms. If religion is, in Ralph Barton Perry's definition, "man's profoundest solicitude for that which he counts most valuable," then the

[2]*Agape and Eros* (London, 1939), pp. 476–77.

word "religion" is totally inapplicable in the context of this
concern. For "value" is always "value for me"; and the disinterestedness to which I am summoned in the Gospel is a
disinterestedness in which I surrender all concern about what
is valuable for me, in favor of a sole concern for God and the
neighbor. The double commandment of total love for God and
the neighbor is joined in the Gospels with the necessity of a
new birth: for from what root in the unredeemed self could
such disinterestedness grow? It is no longer a question of
achieving *my* perfection, or winning *my* salvation, or attaining
to *my summum bonum,* for all these are goods for me, and it
is this very concern about what is good for me that I am invited to put away.[3]

It is at this point that Luther proves himself, as Nygren
says, to be "a Copernicus in the sphere of religion." He perceives, following St. Paul, that if the question about salvation
is to be answered it must be stated entirely anew. In a preliminary way one could say that the question is not how I can
attain my salvation, but how I can stop being concerned about
it. As long as I am preoccupied with the issue of my salvation
(which is the perennial issue for religion) I am not yet delivered from the circle of self. More than that; the preoccupation with the issue of salvation precludes a proper love of the
neighbor since in this context the love of the neighbor must be
a means to my final end. In this context too, as we have noted,

[3]Nygren stresses the importance of Luther's contention against Augustine on this
point: maintaining that in Augustine the idea of salvation is not extricated from
the neoplatonic notion of the heavenly ascent, in which God himself is construed to be a good for the self, the supreme good certainly, but still an object
of *my* desiring. Dietrich Bonhoeffer in his *Letters from Prison* makes the same
point when he suggests that it is very doubtful whether Christianity should be
understood as a religion of salvation at all.

the love of God himself is perverted by the self, since God is still the goal and end of my striving, his love a favor to be sought or earned. This is true whether the religious quest be pressed along the road of moralism or of piety. It is trite enough to say that Luther closes the road of good works, as Paul did, knowing that God's love cannot be earned, and that the unredeemed self can make all good works an occasion of pride; but it is also clear that he closed the road of piety, insisting that the most elevated piety (he refers to Plato, Dionysius the Areopagite and Bonaventure) is a form of self-idolatry, since it still reaches after God as a good for the self.

The *sola gratia, sola fide,* at which Luther arrives is not a solution to the religious question: it is the establishment of a new stance in which the religious question is set aside as irrelevant and impossible of answer in religious terms. What Luther finds in the Gospel is that, not only is the religious question posed with such rigor that it becomes humanly and finally unanswerable, but it becomes finally and forever irrelevant. The self-offering of Jesus as the Christ is for him the stooping of the divine Charity to our necessity. It carries the assurance—"while we were yet sinners Christ died for us"— that our dilemma is totally comprehended and compassed by the love of God. Our self-love pales and fades before the love Christ has for us.[4] In the blaze of this divine charity our religious anxiety becomes an absurdity; and worse, a kind of un-

[4]Luther's thought is moving here within a high estimate of the nature and office of Christ which he has in common with the classical Christian tradition. Jesus is of course Messiah, the one-man Israel in the perfection of His obedience: he is also the "man from heaven" of the later Jewish expectation, the Redeemer whom God provides: but more, He is "the Son from the bosom of the Father," the embodiment of the costly love of God for man. It is an old theological question whether this high Christology is a consequence of the Christian perception of what we have in Christ, or whether the sequence is the opposite of that.

faith. For does not the sacrifice of Christ, in which the costly love of God is embodied, carry with it the assurance that we can safely trust our final destiny to His hands: "God has taken care of my salvation," as Luther puts it. Clearly He loves us and has loved us more than we love ourselves, and therefore He cares for our salvation more even than we could care about it. Henceforth, for Luther, any form of religious anxiety is a kind of blasphemy: "no man can do God greater dishonor than not to trust Him," and to be doubtful about our salvation is simply to refuse to take Him at His word. Furthermore, the insurgent love of Christ so spoils the citadel of self that the self's concern is transferred from the good of the self to the will of Christ. Christ reigns where self was—"not I, but Christ in me"—and the paradigm of the authentic Christian impulse is St. Paul's "I could wish myself accursed from Christ for my brethren. . . ." Here is the biblical transcript of Graham Greene's insight that a man's first problem is not to save his own soul but to transcend his own self.

One of the loveliest figures in Luther's writing speaks to this very point: the Bride and Bridegroom symbol in *The Treatise on Christian Liberty:*

> Faith . . . unites the soul with Christ, like a bride with the bridegroom, and from this marriage Christ and the soul become one body, as St. Paul says (Ephesians 5:30). Then the possession of both are in common, whether fortune, misfortune or anything else, so that what Christ has, also belongs to the believing soul, and what the soul has, will belong to Christ. Now Christ has all good things and also salvation: these now belong to the soul. At present the soul bears each trespass and sin upon itself; these will belong to Christ. At this point begins the glad interchange and contest. Because Christ is both God and man,

and has never sinned, and because His sanctity is unconquerable, eternal and almighty, he takes possession of the sins of the
believing soul by virtue of her wedding-ring, i.e. faith, and acts
just as if he had committed them himself. Thus they must be
swallowed up and drowned in Him, for His unconquerable
righteousness is stronger than all sin. Thus the soul is cleansed
from all sins by her dowry, i.e. for the sake of her faith becomes
unembarrassed and unfettered, and endowed with the eternal
righteousness of Christ, her bridegroom. Is that not a happy
household, when Christ, the rich, noble and good bridegroom,
takes the poor, despised, wicked little whore in marriage, sets
her free from all evil, and decks her with all good things?

This is the end of all moralism and of all salvation-piety,
and the beginning of a truly disinterested will. Such love as
Christ has for us swallows up all self-love, and we henceforth
desire for ourselves "no advantage or salvation." Disinterestedness is nourished now from the only root on which in fact
it can grow, which is grateful love. The love of the neighbor
is detached from all concern about the look of our own spiritual physiognomy, from all anxiety about our salvation. It
partakes now of the free and uncoerced love wherewith Christ
has loved us.

This is the heart of what is meant by "justification by faith,"
or rather, salvation by grace through faith: *sola gratia, sola
fide*. It is the gift of God: an unmerited bounty and a profound
ethical resource. "There is no good in the world or out of it,"
says Kant, "save the good will." "And there is no good will,"
says Emil Brunner in the authentic accent of Luther, "save
the will that is rooted in justification by faith." By the transaction of justification the self is *righted*, or *rectified*, to use an
etymological equivalent of *justification*. Christ reigns where
self was, and man is restored from the prison of his auton-

omous selfhood to the spontaneous "new Covenant" relationship to God and the neighbor in which the command to love is
no longer a command, but the free and uncoerced impulse of
the heart.

Of course this restoration is an eschatological event: that is,
its total fulfillment cannot be contained under the conditions
of time and history. In time and history the new man in Christ
is chained to the old man, that "body of death" (Romans
7:24) by which Paul means not the physical body, but the self
in its enslavement to pride and self, and therefore to death:
he is free "in principle," the transformation is begun, but this
side of the restoration of all things (the *eschaton:* the end)
the new man is yoked to the old man, the new self to the old
self, to a body of death in a world subject to death. In Luther's
phrase he is *simul justus et peccator:* he is *justus*, rectified,
righted, in his relation to God; but this does not mean that he
has outgrown the need for forgiveness: it means that he knows
to Whom to go for it. To assert more than this in the present
dispensation would be to plant another and more deadly seed
of pride. Not only so, but it would separate the Christian from
his human brethren, leading him to forget that he without them
cannot be made perfect. What the doctrine of justification
means in the dimension of sociality is that the justified man
becomes a member of the community of the justified which is
the Church, the *communio sanctorum* which is not a community of perfect men, but a community of men who rejoice
that God loves them this side of their perfection, and are united
in a common exultation, a common dependence, and a common
service of the brethren from which all consciousness of merit
is withdrawn.

A large part of the tragedy of modern Protestantism, for all its numerical mass, is that this primal affirmation of the Reformation is conserved and monopolized so largely by the fundamentalist sects. It is of course also conserved in the formularies of the main-line denominations, and imprinted indelibly in the Scriptures which all the Churches use. But it is the sectarians who operate with it, in a degenerate and frozen form in which the liberating witness to justifying grace becomes a formalized cult of salvation. The act of faith, by which according to Luther a man is set free from religious anxiety to a joyous dependence on God "for all things, and also salvation," and by which he is freed from the somber preoccupation with his own destiny for a self-forgetful service of the brethren for Christ's sake: this act of faith becomes itself an anxious "work," on which the attainment of our salvation precariously depends.[5] But this is to bargain with God again, using the coin of faith if not the works, but using coin nevertheless, and so denying the exuberant and unpurchasable love which is veritably embodied in Christ.

Yet while the wholesome doctrine is thus formalized in the sects, the churches which possess the liberating inheritance regard the "imputation" of Christ's righteousness, as Reinhold Niebuhr says,[6] as "both immoral and irrational," so confident is the modern Christian man in his own actual and potential righteousness. So the churches make do with an emasculated piety in which psychological disciplines of self-improvement and self-acceptance do duty for a Gospel, and a conception of

[5] The classical Reformation documents, for example the Westminster Confession of Faith (1648), fear this very thing, this turning of the act of faith into a "work," and warn men against thinking that God imputes "faith alone, the act of believing, or any other evangelical obedience, to them as their righteousness."

[6] In his Preface to Paul Lehmann's *Forgiveness* (New York, 1940).

social progressivism under the disciplines of history and moral
pedagogy takes the place of that radical renovation for which
the Gospel makes provision, and without which man and nature remain bound in affliction and iron. For the conception
of the Church as the *communio sanctorum*, the reconstitution
of the body of mankind around its proper Center, there is sub-
stituted the notion of a sustaining fellowship which will rein-
force the good impulse and discourage the bad. The conception
is not vicious, but the result is misunderstanding within the
Church of the Church's own nature, which is much more
deadly in the end of the day than any assault upon the Church
by its overt enemies.

Yet in the formalized or neglected doctrine of justification
there is a profound resource for meeting the questions which
men of our generation are being forced again to ask.

Koestler's dilemma of a justice which can never be perfectly
joined to compassion; of a justice and a compassion which
make inescapable yet irreconcilable demands: this impossibility of perfection of righteousness is here comprehended,
and the partial obedience which is the best we can accomplish
is sustained and in some sense perfected by the divine charity.
More of what this means we shall examine when we set about
to relate justification to justice.

The connection is clear with Greene's perception that we
are called to love others and not to save ourselves, after the
fashion of the Lord Christ Himself, of whom it was mockingly
said that "he saved others, himself he cannot save": and that
this self-transcending care for the other is nurtured from an
assurance of salvation which is equivalent to an indifference
to it.

And as for Warren's "we love well, but not well enough": that is true and we know it. But in the faith of the Gospel we discover that if we do not love well at least we are well-beloved; and from this fount of grace and gratitude opens the possibility of a love free of perversion and of pride.

There is a correlation between the contemporary question and the Christian answer. Not an exact correlation, because man never shapes precisely his own profoundest questions; and not an obvious correlation, because the Church has so largely lost the trick of articulating the Gospel. But the correlation is there and it is worth exploring. Out on the frontier some promising territory has been opened, by spiritual scouts who have for the time being swung clear of the main body. We turn now to take a look at it.

*Truly no creature hath more cause to put himself
forth in the cause of his God than have I. I have had
plentiful wages beforehand, and I am sure I shall
never earn the least mite.*

OLIVER CROMWELL *Letters and Speeches*

4. *The Ethics of Justification*

Now that we are some way along with this essay, we are
forced to remember that the whole venture is precarious. It
was announced frankly on the title page as *A Twentieth Century Essay on Justification by Faith*. We have Paul Tillich's
authority for speculating that such an attempt at interpretation is hazardous if not foredoomed.

> The idea [of justification by faith] is strange to the man of
> today and even to Protestant people in the churches: indeed, as
> I have over and over again had the opportunity to learn, it is
> so strange to modern man that there is scarcely any way of
> making it intelligible to him.

And a candid and eloquent friend of mine wrote only today
about the present venture: "For God's sake (literally) be
careful about justification by faith: it's the biggest escape
mechanism in history."

This last I find a little difficult to take, since both my friend
and I come of a long line of escape merchants from Luther
through Calvin and Knox to Niemöller and Berggrav: but it is
clear that the doctrine is both alien, and, where the sound of
it at least is known, disquieting.

So far we have dealt somewhat obliquely with the matter, finding adumbrations of the doctrine in the writings of some of the most influential of contemporary spokesmen, and suggesting that their problems are anticipated in the Hebrew-Christian scriptures. Now that we come to deal with it more explicitly, there is some reassurance in the fact that we are to handle it in close relation to the problems of conduct: for even "the Protestant people in the churches," while they may make little of the Pauline discussions of justification even when they read them, and may make less of the classical formulations of the Reformation which shaped their churches, are nothing if not moral (in the best sense) and moralistic (in the worst sense). Religion to be relevant must be practical, so the popular and not un-American argument runs. It must illumine and enable men at the point of ethical decision, stiffening the moral fiber, bringing life into some kind of moral order and keeping it there. Outside of the holiness groups which still make play with salvation formulae, the preferred emphasis is upon the "plain moral teaching" of Christianity. The paraphernalia of doctrine and liturgy are to be borne with since they appear to be inevitable concomitants of moral instruction; but their place is peripheral at best, while at worst they are no doubt assumed to be priestly and ministerial adornments of the simple gospel, whose essential content *must* be moral, since what a man most needs for the practical business of living is plainly and simply to be told what he ought to do.

At a more responsible and sophisticated level, a generation which may find the traditional formulae strange and dark, may yet be assumed to find itself at grips with difficult and ambiguous moral decisions in the sphere both of personal and political life. The scientist, the businessman and the working politician, if they have any degree of moral sensitivity, have it also in common that they lie awake nights measuring the human consequences of their necessary activity. They may even have noticed that for their diverse dilemmas the simpler formulae seem to leave a good deal out. It is tempting to reduce religion to "the Fatherhood of God and the Brotherhood of Man," which is the working faith of many; but it is not clear how this illumines, without further articulation and interpretation, the question of whether to make or not to make the Bomb, or the intricacies of operating the wheat exchange, or the problem of whether to fight or not to fight for Korea or Quemoy.

As I meet the ethical issue most directly—apart from the daily business of trying to keep a Christian course myself—it is in the form of undergraduate questions. I teach Christian ethics—Heaven help me!—and I find that the students who take my classes state the issue somewhat in this form: they have acquired in the nurture of home and church a set of standards (they have learned to call them *mores*) which served them well enough through the callow years, but which now are sharply challenged by the prevailing mores of the fraternity or the campus *set*. Widening perspectives and a year in Sociology I make them aware of the qualified character of the family group, and the provisional character of its standards. They find themselves sinking in a morass of moral relativity, and they want firm standing ground. Their assumption is that a professional Christian teacher exists and gets paid to provide precisely that: a firm and self-validating set of "values" which will put an end to moral dubiety, bring conflicting mores into some kind of order, and take every element of precariousness out of the ethical life. And just as it is assumed that the available certainties are either logical or experimental, so in this area it is assumed that Christian values must be vindicated either rationally or scientifically, with no remaining room for doubt.

At this point there are certain sure ways to create immediate alarm and despondency. One has to point out, for example, that the word *values* which is assumed to be the stock-in-trade of all ethical discussion not only has the boring quality of all abstractions, but that it also is a word unknown to the biblical tradition, which deals not in abstractions but in the concreteness of covenant and compact, of love and loyalty. Again, it is worth emphasizing, at the risk of further initial confusion, that the moral life as we live it and the moral judgment as we make it are set in a context of incoherence and illogicality; for our most profound revulsions—against torture for example—and our most eager approbations—for example, of the four chaplains who gave up their life belts and went down with the World War II transport—are alike without logical ground or scientific validation.

The root of the trouble here, and of much confusion everywhere, is the traditional identification of Christian ethics with rational ethics, especially and regularly with absolute, idealist ethics. This has so seeped into the minds of our Christian-trained youngsters that they are incapable of carrying on a discussion with the ethical relativists in theory, or of living with the relativities of social life in practice. It is more than time that Christian ethics were once and for all distinguished from all forms of rational idealism and from every kind of absolutism. For biblical ethics like biblical religion stand on their own essential ground, and are to be confused neither with rational ethics nor with the ethics of calculation, neither with idealism nor pragmatism. What then *are* the ethics which derive from biblical faith?

Historically and philosophically there are, very broadly speaking, two possible approaches to the problems of conduct. They correspond to the two religious options which, as we have seen, biblical religion characteristically avoids. Koestler's *Yogi* and *Commissar* symbols not only correspond to two types of world outlook, but they also stand representative of the two perennial options in ethical thinking. The *Commissar* represents an ethic of pure calculation, the *Yogi* that of pure compassion. They correspond, as we noticed, to the two perennial options in the sphere of religion: the deification of the vitalities of nature and history, or the attempted transcendence of these dynamisms in sheer abstraction from the world. Koestler's problem is that pure compassion cannot implement itself in action and so passes into contemplative withdrawal; while the ethic of calculation which is designed to maximize the human good by efficient social engineering degenerates, without the restraint of compassion, into sheer nihilistic ruthlessness.

Historically speaking, of course, neither of these options is ever found pure. Natural religion and world-renouncing spirituality tend as we have seen to pass into each other according as men look *at* nature or look *through* it, find it fascinating or revolting: and since as Koestler sees it the final consequences of either course tend to be humanly intolerable, in life and in fact men's moral behavior is less tidy than any simple theory can account for. It is notorious for example that Kant's absolute ethic of conscience can connect itself with the real world of decision and action only by importing the most blatant element of calculation ("Act only on that maxim which you can will to become a Universal Law of Nature"), and the Marxists, who attempt an ethic of pure calculation of the greatest good of the greatest number, end by sacrificing indefinite numbers to a purely formal historical and social dogma.

Just as the Bible avoids both natural religion and world-renunciation, so it surefootedly avoids both the purely prudential and the purely rational, abstract types of ethical thinking. It knows nothing of idealism *or* of pragmatism. But before we attempt to set out the biblical faith in its relation to conduct, it is worth noticing that in point of fact both the rational and pragmatic views of ethics stand far removed from the etymological meaning of the word. For *ethics* relates to *ethos*, just as *morals* are tied to *mores*, and these etymological connections suggest a social origin and a social character for moral standards which are too little taken account of either by the rationalists or the pragmatists, and might seem at first to give comfort to the ethical relativists, who emphasize the socially conditioned and provisional character of all "values."

There is an increasing volume of Christian writing on the problems of conduct which is not only content but concerned that the ethics derived from biblical faith should be discriminated once and for all from rational idealism (with its correlative *natural law*) and would argue that they can be so separated without falling into pure relativism. Here, for example, is Professor Paul Lehmann of Princeton on *The Foundation and Pattern of Christian Behaviour.*[1]

> Christian ethics, as a theological discipline, has to do with the "ethos" of Christians. The word "ethos" is derived from a Greek verb *eiotha* meaning "to be accustomed to." The idea is that what one is accustomed to gives stability to the human situation and thus makes conduct possible and meaningful. By some such correspondence between language and reality, "ethos," as a noun, meant "dwelling" or "stall." What was originally referred to animals as giving stability and security to their existence came also to be applied to human relations. So, the ethos of a society denotes that which gives stability and security to human behavior. Ethos is, so to say, the cement of human society. . . .

"The cement of society" . . . but of what society? For every type of human society tends to generate its own ethics—the family, the fraternity, the nation, each attempts to impose its own standards, and that is precisely where the problem lies. Let's take one representative out of my undergraduate constituency. This girl, a charmer and much in demand, was tormented about a conflict in sex standards between her home training and the campus mores. The boys, she said, expected heavy petting as a normal part of campus dating, and from this she revolted. But her concern was that as a rational modern she could give no rational reason for this revulsion, either to herself or to others. And again the assumption was that there must *be* some rational reason, and that it was the business of the Christian moralist to provide it. So I asked her to tell me,

[1] In *Christian Faith and Social Action*, John A. Hutchison, Editor (Scribners, 1953).

off the top of her head, what seemed to her to be the real ground of her resistance. "It's too silly," said she, "but I suppose it's because my mother told me not to!" Now it seems to me that my first business was to point out that this reason is by no means as silly as, to a rational modern, it sounds: for what she really meant was that in the community of her first loyalty she had learnt standards of restraint and self-possession, to deny which would be to loosen her loyalty to that primal community, and to break confidence. That is clearly not the end of the matter, since on this and more important issues she must find some stance from which she could evaluate and correct the provisional standards of the home. But would this new stance be a self-validating rational standard?

In point of fact, from the viewpoint of biblical faith, No. For biblical ethics are not rational ethics, just as biblical faith is not a variety of rational idealism. And what the Christian moralist can offer is not a self-validating rational standard, but a community of loyalty which transcends and holds in some sort of proportion and relation the loyalty to home and to peer-group and to nation, and whatever other communities of loyalty lay demands upon us.

Let us be more precise about this. "Christian ethics, as a theological discipline, has to do with the *ethos* of Christians." Which is another way of saying that biblical ethics are covenant ethics, just as biblical religion is covenant religion. The revelatory events which were crucial for Israel's history, which brought the community of faith into being, by the same token created a community *ethos*, a set of community *mores*. We have seen this illustrated at two points: in the first place the *Law* of the Hebrews is a transcript of the community's understanding of its own life in relation to the God who claimed the community for his own in the Sinai-event; and the *Prophetic Witness*, as we have noticed, appeals not to a private and personal, mystical or rational, disclosure, but to the loyalty which is involved in being a member of the community at all, as it lives its life in relation to the God of love and righteousness. Biblical ethics, that is to say, are neither rational nor experimental, neither idealist nor pragmatic: they are community ethics. In New Testament terms they are *koinonia* (fellowship) ethics, as the essay of Paul Lehmann's already referred to makes emphatically clear. He quotes *The Letter to the Ephesians:*

> . . . we are meant to hold firmly to the truth in love, and to grow up in everything into Christ the Head. For it is from the Head that the whole Body, as an harmonious structure knit together by the joints with which it is provided, grows by the proper functioning of individual parts to its full maturity in love. . . . Live life, then, with a due sense of responsibility, not as men who do not know the meaning and purpose of life but as those who do . . ."[2]

And that is always the sequence of the New Testament argument. "If God so loved us, we ought also to love one another." There is not, to put it baldly, a trace of rationalism or experimentalism in it. It is ethics (*ethos*) in the strict and forgotten sense. It calls a community to a "style" of life consonant with its origin and nature. The Christians are summoned to live as the sons of God they are, to behave like members of that *koinonia* which is the costly fruit of God's self-offering in Christ, the reconstituted family of mankind.

[2]Ephesians 4–5. As in J. B. Phillips, *Letters to Young Churches* (Macmillan, New York, 1950).

This means in practical fact that in the face of the confusion of standards, the conflict of mores, which torments the undergraduate and the modern world, what the Christian faith has to offer is not a set of rational standards rationally perceived, but *another set of mores,* the mores of the Church (*koinonia*) or better, the mores of the Kingdom of God. The Christian faith need not at all be taken aback by the assertion that ethical standards are social products, that all ethics are *relational* ethics.[3] From the biblical and Christian point of view the question, of course, is, in what context of relations is the discussion carried on? Does it have an authentic center and sufficient scope, or is it distorted and idolatrous, or distorted because it is idolatrous?

The concern of biblical faith is not the sanctification of the world or any part of it, or the transcendence of the world, but the organization of the world around its true and authentic center, which is God the Creator and Redeemer, the God of love and righteousness, who is the God of Abraham, Isaac and Jacob, the God and Father of our Lord Jesus Christ. And this God as we have seen is not a rational principle, but the Creator of community and that community's living focus of love and loyalty. It is within this community of faith that there are generated the mores which transcend and correct all provisional and local standards. Since, however, this community is constituted not by rational agreement but by living and personal

[3]H. Richard Niebuhr of Yale in an important essay *The Center of Value* (in *Moral Principles of Action,* Ruth Nanda Anshen, Editor, Harper, 1952) argues that in practice all ethics are relational ethics, and that the frank recognition that this is so is not only entirely congenial to Christianity, which has too long been confused with idealism, but would open a fruitful debate between Christianity and the naturalists. The importance of this is clear, for example, as it affects our attitude to a frankly relational value theory like that of Ralph Barton Perry, in which values are "objects of interest."

loyalty to the One God, its *ethics* constitute not a set of rational and formal principles, but a mesh of obligations determined by the relation of one member of the Community to another, and of all to the community's Head.

Christian ethics in this sense are inseparable from the peculiar biblical understanding of salvation and justification. To be justified is to have life *rectified*, so that it is not organized around the false and idolatrous center of the self (nor around any enlarged or expanded idolatrous self such as family or nation) but moves upon its true and authentic fulcrum. The other side of the transaction is justification, wherein the citadel of self is ravaged and Christ reigns where self was, all that is done is done, as Luther says, "simply to please God thereby." And what pleases God most, as the New Testament makes abundantly clear, is the simple and selfless service of the neighbor, in the most practical fashion and the most down-to-earth way. This is that "Faith active in Love," which is the slogan form of Reformation ethics, and whose content has to be rediscovered and relived in every generation and in every situation.

The difficulty is to put content into it without falling again into the legalism of rationalism, or into pure pragmatism. The most massive and influential attempt at it in our generation is probably Emil Brunner's *The Divine Imperative*.[4] Brunner begins by affirming the authentic starting point of Christian ethics, in comment on Kant: "There is no good will save that which is rooted in justification by faith," and goes on to discuss in the most detailed and illuminating fashion how such good will will implement itself in the natural communities of

[4]The Westminster Press, Philadelphia, 1947.

family, labor, economics, politics and culture. But he runs into difficulty; and instead of holding to the question how in all these relationships the human good may be maximized, he falls back upon rational and "natural" criteria of what that good must be. He rests his case for monogamy, for example, in part upon the alleged fact that it is primitive (and therefore "natural") or alternatively that it is late, historically and sociologically speaking, and has the tendency to assert itself over alternative forms of sexual organization. Now these facts, in so far as they are facts, may have their importance as illustrating the necessities of the human case, but they do not make a "Law." For from the Christian point of view the good is defined neither by what is early nor by what is late, by what is rational or by what is natural, but by what is good for man. There is an element of thoroughgoing pragmatism in Christian ethics, which is more fully taken account of in the work of Reinhold Niebuhr, in particular in *An Interpretation of Ethics*,[5] in which the Christian life of faith and obedience is set explicitly between the love-commandment which is the quintessence of the divine Law and defines the life of the community of the justified, and the necessities of the practical case.

If we use that starting point ourselves, what do we find?

We might begin here by noticing certain points of comparison and contrast with extra-biblical ethics both rational and experimental, both philosophic and scientific.

Broadly speaking it is clear that any form of absolute ethics, either of the rational sort or in the form of Kant's ethic of conscience, tends to care more for motives than for conse-

[5]Harper and Brothers, New York, 1935.

quences; while a pragmatic ethic (e.g., Marxism) manifestly cares more for consequences than for motives. The point of view on motives and consequences which stems from biblical faith is somewhat more complex than either of these. The biblical concern about the divine righteousness is a concern not only that the wills of men be rightly oriented, but that the affairs of the world be rightly ordered. This involves a preoccupation both with motives *and* with consequences. Now it may be argued that over motives we have some sort of control, but that consequences are frequently incalculable and therefore such a calculation cannot be decisive at the point of ethical decision. Modern psychology would teach us to be wary of any certainty about motives, either our own or those of other people. They are regularly as undiscoverable as consequences are incalculable. The fact is that we can neither pinpoint motives nor calculate consequences with any precision (cf. Peter Slavek in Koestler's *Arrival and Departure*), so that while we are bound to try to clarify motives and estimate consequences, at both the internal and external boundary of ethical action we are thrown upon the mercy of God, without whom "nothing is true, nothing is perfect." We shall be concerned more precisely with this matter in later discussion of political choice; but we might mark here a saying of Dietrich Bonhoeffer[6] in his *Letters from Prison:*

> To say that we are justified by faith and not by success is a very different thing from saying that we can be indifferent to success or failure.

[6]Bonhoeffer, whom we have referred to earlier, was a Protestant theologian of great devotion and penetration who spent two yars in Hitler's prisons, had a part in the plot on Hitler's life, and was hanged on the eve of possible rescue by the Americans.

There is in Christian ethics both an absolute element *and* an element of calculation: but Christian ethics differ from idealist ethics in that the absolute is an absolute loyalty and not an absolute principle, while the Christian calculation differs from typical pragmatism in that, while there is always a hidden absolute in pragmatism, an unadmitted presupposition about what is good for man, in the Christian scheme the calculation is grounded in a very precise understanding of what is good for man, determined by the revelation of God in Christ: "Live life, then," says St. Paul, "not as men who do not know the meaning and purpose of life but as those who do."

It is possible now to set out the elements which enter into a Christian ethical decision, which is not made on the basis of a deduction from rational principle, as in the characteristic "natural law" fashion, nor on the basis of "pure expediency."

A valid Christian decision is compound always of both *faith* and *facts*. It is likely to be valid in the degree to which the faith is rightly apprehended and the facts are rightly measured. It is the product, that is to say, of an absolute loyalty related to a pragmatic choice. Its precondition is a prayerful conformity in thought and life to "the truth as it is in Jesus," with all that this involves of profound submission to the mind of Christ in the Gospel, and the will of Christ to create for himself a community of brethren out of the separated individuals and the sundered communities of mankind: that first of all. But this does not provide the necessary ingredients of decision. It is to be noted that none of the "ethical sayings of Jesus" are actually prescriptive of conduct: rather they define the character of the new community into which men are brought by submission to the truth of the Gospel. But to be told to love our neighbor as ourselves, salutary and exacting as it is, does not resolve the question whether to go into Korea or to stay out, or define the precise degree of compromise necessary for political participation. For such daily decisions the faith must be conjoined to the facts, and what the faith does is not to alter the shape of the facts, but to tutor us to estimate them with disinterested precision, so that we may manipulate them to the maximum human and social good. This is, I take it, what Karl Barth means when he urges Christians to "sleep neither over their Bibles nor over their newspapers." For while the Bible is the source from which our faith is nurtured, in which the *ethos* of the kingdom of God is best communicated, the newspapers represent our access to hard and secular fact, the kind of fact which determines the form of our contemporary decision, the raw material for the sanctification of life.[7]

It should be added here that while the faith does not alter the facts, it does alter the dimension in which they are seen, and the depth with which they are comprehended. Statistics about living standards, for example, while they do not change in Christian hands, do become the bearers of a human content and a weight of anguish, so that it may be that caloric content, if it means starvation, represents for the Christian not simply an arithmetical symbol for intellectual comprehension, but a profound demand for costly identification with the brethren for whom Christ died. One should say then that a valid Christian ethical decision is compound not only of faith and facts, but involves a real process of *identification*, which welds faith to facts in the same movement which unites us to

[7]Barth's reference to the newspapers I take to be symbolic and not naïve. He is as well aware as the next man that it is necessary not only to read them, but to notice who owns them!

our brother men. "And this I pray," wrote Paul to the Philippians, "that your *love* may abound more and more in *knowledge* and in all *judgment*."[8] Love in this context is a synonym for faith: the knowledge which arms faith for action includes knowledge of the relevant facts; but the judgment or the insight which Paul craves for the Christians is generated when the facts are brought into relation to the faith, and so yield their full human meaning.

Does all this mean, as it seems to mean, that every ethical decision must be approached *de novo*, without the guidance of any general principles at all? In a sense it does mean that. But it does not mean that we are left without the kind of resources which rational and general ethical principles are supposed to provide. We are delivered from legalism, but we are not surrendered to individualism. We may have to live life without general principles, but we do have the resources of a cumulative inheritance. The community to whose *ethos* or *mores* we are concerned to conform, which has its life from Christ and its charter from the Scriptures, is a living community of faith, in whose corporate experience most of the problems we confront have been up for decision either in the precise form in which we meet them, or in forms not unrelated to our contemporary dilemma. Communities not only generate mores, they form habits. And just as any wholesome family inculcates habits of restraint and consideration which condition conduct, so the ongoing life of the Christian *koinania* fosters a life of such a style and shape that it predetermines conduct in many a representative situation. This does not mean that all Church habits are good ones, but it does mean that when bad habits

[8]Philippians 1:9. Italics ours.

are formed within the Church, as they regularly are, the best resource for their correction is within the tradition of the Church itself, in the recollection of its primal origin and of its original charter.

Another question of real importance immediately arises. Does not this determination of Christian conduct in terms of a community *ethos* set the Christian too far apart from other men of good will and destroy the basis for co-operation with such men on matters of common ethical concern? And does it not discount the extent to which the life and conviction of such men of good will parallels and even excels the record of Christian men both in clarity of ethical conviction and integrity of ethical life?

The traditional view has been that the agreement on matters of conduct between Christians and non-Christians, for example their common convictions about the urgencies of social justice, presupposes some rational or natural law, known to all rational men, and independent of the specific nurture of the Christian community. Now the agreement is there and to be cherished. But what does it really imply? Does the fact that Christians and non-Christians commend the costly sacrifice of the four chaplains means that either Christians or non-Christians can give rational grounds for it? Or does it mean simply that our revulsion against cruelty and selfishness, and the lifting up of our heart in the face of heroic compassion, are part of our human constitution, reinforced by our recognition that the human community is impoverished by the one and enriched by the other? It seems to me that most of what is traditionally attributed to rational natural law can be accounted for by the recognition of the necessities of human society on the one hand, and on the other by an innate compassion (sometimes hard put to it to find rational justification) which may wage an uneasy and uncertain war against our latent egoism, yet is powerful enough to put its impress upon our common mind, upon our tradition and upon our institutions. In this sense, as Paul says, men without the Law do by nature the things contained in the Law: but the Law as Paul knows it is not the law of reason but the law of Moses, the mores of the believing community: and the "nature" which holds men to compassion and to justice is not rational nature as the Greeks thought, but human nature which carries compassion at times beyond the bounds of reason. The residual image of God? Maybe. In any event it is ground for rejoicing from the Christian camp, and sufficient ground for a working ethical agreement along most of the road where Christians walk with others.

In the early stages of this study we turned up some ethical test questions by which we may measure now what resources our view of ethics puts at our service for the handling of the contemporary problem. What do we Christians make, for example, of Koestler's Yogi and Commissar dilemma, not in theory but in practice?

We have some clinical experience of this problem in the experience of Christians of our own generation. For the same experiences which set the problem for Koestler were shared in by Christians using precisely the resources of faith which we have been trying to recover. Some of the most illuminating material in this connection comes out of the European Resistance of World War II, which forced both Roman Catholic and Protestant Christians to assess conventional attitudes and reach for the profoundest Gospel insight upon precisely Koestler's problem. If the Christian men of the Resistance did not know before they committed themselves, they very soon learned that to participate in the anti-Nazi struggle was to be plunged into a moral maelstrom, in which no rules would help. For to resist one must stay alive, and to stay alive one must forge and cheat. Ration books and passports must be forged or stolen. Even within the Christian group, the traitor or the potential traitor must be liquidated without hesitation if not without compunction, since not only might the lives of the group members depend upon it, but the good cause itself. But drive this to its logical limit, and where does it take us? Presumably if a man may be liquidated as a danger to the good cause, the same man may be tortured to make him yield information vital to the good cause. If he resists torture himself, might it not be effective and therefore necessary to torture his children before his eyes? Without doubt many honest Nazis, like many honest Communists, used this kind of argument and resorted to torture with real veracity of motive. Torquemada's inquisitors were not dishonest men, nor necessarily vicious beyond the rest of us. Within a certain frame of reference—or lacking a certain frame of reference—this is irrefutable logic, and it has been salutary in these last years to listen to Christians who had to weigh the force of it.

I recall putting precisely these questions in 1945 to a group of French and Dutch Christians who had just come out of the Resistance. Forgery, lying and liquidation: they had had a hand in all of them. Then, said I, is *everything* permitted? The reply was quite clear and quite crucial: "Yes: everything is permitted—and everything is forbidden." In other words, if

killing and lying are to be used it must be under the most
urgent pressure of social necessity, and with a profound sense
of guilt that no better way can presently be found. That is at
least a sure safeguard against carrying on torture, for example, just for the fun of the thing, as Nazism and other
nihilisms would permit. Of course it is possible to refuse the
whole calculation and avoid involvement: but I think I prefer
the tone and temper of a Christian member of the French Resistance who wrote as he went underground:

> I ask God, too, that He now forgive me my sins, and the deci-
> sion which I voluntarily take this day (for I know that recourse
> to violence has need of pardon). But I am leaving without hate
> and fully convinced that we Christians have not the right to
> leave it to non-Christians alone to offer their lives.

The faith and the facts, the absolute loyalty and the precarious
calculation, a venture upon uncertain motives and incalculable
consequences: the Resistance situation is the extreme case but
the characteristic form of Christian decision. But notice that
the dire decisions which are here involved, while they are not
held under the neat restraint of any moral formula, are held
under the restraint of Christian compassion. And what good
in any event would a formula do? It is in every normal case a
bad thing to lie, because it corrodes confidence and breaks
community. But from the same group of anti-Nazi fighters I
heard of a case in which Jewish refugees from Hitler were
being transported to Britain in fishing boats from a North Sea
port. On one particular evening the human cargo was aboard
and the little ship was waiting for the tide, when a Nazi patrol
came by on the dock. They knew the captain well but made a
perfunctory inquiry about what he was carrying. Should the

reply then have been: "Four Jewish adults, and seven children of diverse ages"? Or does the faith commend compassion, which cannot be guaranteed never to be at war with verbal veracity? "There is none good but One, that is, God": and no rational formula, no legalistic principle, can be idolatrously elevated to His place. As the captain said in the film of *The Cruel Sea*, in anguish of mind after getting a U-boat at the cost of dropping a depth-charge among his own comrades struggling in the sea: "I suppose you must just go on and do what you have to do—and say your prayers."

We shall have to discuss the vexed question of ends and means more directly when we come to the political issue. The question is clearly latent here. But at this point we can say this much: that what the Christian *ethos* or the Christian spirit requires of us is that we allow ourselves to be tutored by the faith and submitted to the facts: and that since our grasp of the faith is always unsure and our mastery of the facts always partial and limited; since we can neither assess our motives with confidence nor calculate consequences with certainty, we are cast in the end always on the forbearance and forgiveness of God. But is that not part of what justification by faith means?

Love of the brethren is good citizenship.

Justice is the hard, general and rational skeleton of community indwelt by sin.

A. T. MOLLEGEN, in *Anglican Evangelicalism*

5. *Justification and Justice*

It is very generally taken for granted in the present Christian generation that the faith is to be related to the social facts. It is only in minority and sectarian groups that the Christian Gospel is interpreted in a purely individualistic and "perpendicular" fashion: and since those groups of necessity have part and lot in the economic-political melee, they normally take over an uncritical political conventionalism and conservatism. This in itself is anomalous: partly because the early sectarianism both in Europe and in Britain had a strongly revolutionary thrust and partly because the contemporary sectarians themselves retain closer connection with the dispossessed than does the main-line Church. The main body of Protestant Christianity, on the other hand, while it pays lip service to the relevance of Christian faith to social life, normally works out this connection pretty much in terms of human and social idealism, without any particular relation to the complex of biblical faith, still less to the particular doctrine of justification by faith.

Our present concern is to take a look at some of the less dramatic but still urgent necessities of social life, and to try to get a biblical grip on them. Part of our problem is that the political-economic content of the Bible is very largely closed territory to the member of the "church-on-the-corner." The bold and massive constructions of Christian social theology which are the work for example of Reinhold Niebuhr and Emil Brunner are not everybody's meat, and the best-seller lists are consistently topped by mere inanities. The Bible itself, over a large part of Protestantism, is simply not read. Many of our ministers and congregations do not pay the canonical Scriptures even the minimum respect of reading them as they were written, in a consistent and continuous and reasonably complete fashion. Instead the pastor feels criminally free to select passages coinciding with his sermonic predilections: so that, while most congregations know the sound at least of the more immediately edifying passages like I Corinthians 13 (generally out of context), any man who chooses to read the strong warnings of the Deuteronomic Law against monopoly, or our Lord's salutary sayings about riches, may be suspect as subversive if not Communist. Yet the content of the Law, which is so largely economic-political, carries as full canonical authority as do the more pious-sounding and congenial passages. The most urgent single reform which contemporary Protestantism needs is the requirement that in public worship the Bible be read as it is written, and that preaching be consistently bound to the biblical word. How else will it ever be learned or relearned that piety and politics belong together, as do justice and justification?

For as we have already seen, the Bible in its consistent

witness stands clear both of detached and non-political spirituality and of religious individualism. It treats of a divine righteousness which touches man's life in every dimension: internal and external, spiritual and material, personal and social. "In the beginning God created the heavens *and the earth* . . . ," and both the Law and the Cult which seal and signify the demand of the divine righteousness are designed to set man's life in a firm context of community obligation, and in a responsible relation to the material world. Biblical spirituality, as we have necessarily insisted, is not an indifference to the material but its true and godly use. Biblical holiness is not detached piety, but is both etymologically connected and strictly related to the *whole*some ordering of man's relations with man in the Covenanted and faithful community. The witness of the Hebrew prophetic movement no matter where you touch it is in large part a protest against an ungodly "spirituality" which finds the material demands of the divine Law onerous, and would substitute therefor a detached and socially indifferent cultism, making sacrifice do duty for justice. But, say the prophets with one insistent voice, not a multitude of rams or ten thousand rivers of sacrificial oil can close the ear of the Almighty to the cry of the neglected poor. The smoke of the sacrifice which is made substitute for justice stinks in the nostrils of the Most High.

The Deuteronomic Law, which is a product of the prophetic movement, ranges over the whole reach of man's social life, noting those practices which break the human community and divide man from man, in specific the withholding of the goods of the earth which are given for man's necessities; condemning the monopoly in land and in wheat which is the apparatus of exploitation; putting every detail of social-commercial dealing —like the payment of wages and procedures in the matter of debt—under the scrutiny of an implacable and compassionate righteousness.

In the New Testament this exhaustive delineation of what the divine holiness requires is not reiterated but taken for granted. The new Law of the Gospel is the quintessence of the old, rid of exception and qualification. The act of faith which sets a man within the new Community is an act of exultant solidarity, wholly spurious unless it issues in the feeding of the hungry and the clothing of the naked.

What the New Testament faith does is to root the solidarity of mankind, as one redeemed Body, in the embodied love of God in Christ. The community of the justified men, in whom the circle of self is broken, is the community of those who, being "righted" with God, are set in a relation of joyous obligation with all "the brethren for whom Christ died." This new solidarity implements itself first within the *koinonia*— "neither counted any man aught that he possessed to be his own"—but it shortly runs out into political concern and the care of the state, as soon as it becomes manifest that the community of love must coexist with the communities of law, and that the feeding of the hungry and the care of the poor is a political act. It is this coexistence of the community of love with the community of law, and the perception that the law of justice, like the Law of God, can be an instrument of love, that sets the problem for Christian political thought.

The problem is always misunderstood when the Christian faith is construed too simply as a religion of salvation. For in that case political work is necessarily indifferent, since "You can't save men by act of Congress"; or else political work becomes one aspect of the work of salvation, directed to spiritual rather than to plain and practical ends. We ought to look at each of these distortions.

Political indifference is far less characteristic of contemporary Christianity than political wrongheadedness, but the "act of Congress" formula does serve still to justify political inaction, and it is worth a word. Of course you can't save men by act of Congress, if by that is meant that no form or bulk of legislation will reconcile man to God and man to man in the selfless solidarity which is wrought out of the mystery of grace alone. But it is the very recognition that salvation is *sola gratia*, *sola fide* which lifts that Christian man out of his preoccupation with salvation (which can neither be manipulated for himself or for others) and frees him for disinterested service. Men are not *saved* by act of Congress, but they are *served* by good legislation and victimized by bad. No political procedure will get a man to Heaven, but valid political procedures will free him from tyranny and exploitation, maximize freedom and minimize want, and accomplish many another good work which the Law of God requires. Even the "cup of cold water," the New Testament symbol of compassion, in our complex modern world has a plain political meaning. Not many summers ago, in New York, the city was in dire straits for water because the level of the dams was at an unprecedented low. The supply of water for seven million people was threatened for lack, as it would seem, of an adequate dam and reticulation system. At one stage back this becomes a political question: it becomes a question of honest and diligent city government, free from graft and free from the

kind of immediate pressures which inhibit long-term plan-
ning. The symbol of compassion becomes a symbol of political
obligation, an obligation as urgent as the Evangel: for in the
Gospel the cup of cold water, the feeding of the hungry and
the clothing of the naked, is close-yoked with the act of faith
and with the preaching of the Gospel itself, the one no less
urgent than the other.

The opposite distortion does not neglect political work as
indifferent to salvation, but construes political work as part
of the work of salvation. But it springs from the same false
notion that salvation is a work to be accomplished and not a
gift to be received. I take two illustrations of this distortion,
one political, one social-economic:

1. Roman Catholic theology, entangled since Augustine
with the *eros*-mysticism of Hellenism and the philosophic quest
of salvation, and wedded to the notion that "a man's first business is to save his own soul," finds it difficult to construe the
state's function save as part of the work of salvation. And
Roman Catholic state theory has been subject to recurrent distortion stemming precisely from here. For since the state is
manifestly not organized for the work of salvation, its service
of salvation is almost necessarily construed, and historically
has been construed, as service of the Church. This means in
practice that Roman Catholicism tends to judge rulers (Franco
is a contemporary case) by their piety rather than by their
strict service of justice. The Reformation tradition is warned
by its formularies against this very perversion. The confes-
sional statements of the churches of the Reformation again and
again insist that the magistrate's "infidelity" or "unbelief"

do not disqualify him for the office of magistrate, since his prime business is to foster justice rather than piety. They still give the civil authorities larger prerogatives than we would think wholesome in respect of the care of the Church and the preservation of sound doctrine; but they do separate the state's work explicitly from the work of salvation, which is the work of God by the witness of His Church.

The test of states, that is to say, is whether they do that work of God which properly belongs to them, which is the work of justice, rather than whether they make formal acknowledgment of the God whose work they do. Yet there is a chronic tendency to judge political aspirants and political officials by their piety rather than by their proven capacity to serve the common interest. I talked in 1948 with a Protestant church official in England whom I had known well during World War II, and from whom I was seeking impressions of the Labour Government, for I had been out of the country since the Labour Party took office in 1945. To my astonishment, for I had already looked the situation over, he was violently and almost hysterically critical. The freedom of the Church was gone, said he. And when I asked him for chapter and verse, he pointed to the fact that the government's regulations in respect of labor and building materials, and their control of land transfer, made it impossible for the Church to build new buildings "when and where it had the money to pay for them." Now it seemed to me patent that in the postwar situation in Britain, with a million houses down, labor and material short, and both the need and the opportunity for large scale replanning, any government worth its salt must insist on some order of priority, and some right to "clear" new projects. The Church in such a situation had no more right to build new churches at its sweet will than had J. Arthur Rank to build new cinemas. To claim such a right seemed to me to be to separate the interests of piety too sharply from the interests of justice; and to judge the state in such a way, by its friendliness to the Church, was to fall back into the error from which the Lord by the Reformation had once delivered us.

2. An economic instance of the same distortion appears in many discussions of the much-discussed Welfare State. The notorious social backwardness of Roman Catholic countries is not unrelated to a theological error. I have noticed in Dublin, for example, how normal measures of welfare, like old-age pensions, have been restricted by the Church insistence that for the state to accept the care of the old is spiritually unwholesome for the young, since it delivers them from the necessity of looking after their own aged. Now there is something salutary about this care for the stability and solidarity of the family, but the actual human effect in the slum areas of Dublin is that both young and old are embittered (and overcrowded) by the old people's penury and dependency. The cause may be in part in the poverty of the country; but the faulty theological logic is present and potent. In a more general way it is to be noticed that there is considerable hierarchical resistance to welfare measures of every sort, on the ground, sometimes made quite explicit, that any general program of welfare will "dry up the springs of private charity." But it is neither implied in the Gospel nor is it politically hopeful to argue that the poor must be present to help save the souls

of the rich: nor is this perverse logic given authority by responsible contemporary Roman Catholic teaching.

But it persists in Protestantism. I recall going back to New Zealand, where my home was, after the Welfare State in a comprehensive form had been in existence for about ten years. A buoyant export market and a managed distribution of the proceeds of prosperity had eliminated any kind of poverty for that whole decade. The human results were interesting and, as one would surmise, mixed. But a characteristic Christian and Protestant comment alarmed me not a little. It implied that since unremitting prosperity had brought problems of incentive and problems of waste it would be all to the good, piously and spiritually speaking, if we could have just a touch of depression for our souls' sake. The argument is peculiarly unimpressive and not a little offensive when it comes from a pious middle class reasonably well cushioned against recession. It was argued only recently, in a meeting of the National Council of Presbyterian Men (U.S.A.) that to allow the state to extend its prerogatives in the sphere of welfare was to allow the state "to do God's work for Him." It's enough to turn the ancestors of contemporary Presbyterianism—from Paul through Luther to Calvin—in their already unquiet graves: for Luther and Calvin, to take characteristic and influential examples, believed of the state that it was set up precisely to do God's work for Him, in the implementation of social justice. This or that measure of social welfare may be wholesome or unwholesome, discreet or indiscreet, but the notion that God's prerogatives are necessarily infringed when the state's prerogatives are extended has no sanction in Reformation theology at all.

The long and consistent tradition of Christian thought still has the right of the matter: that the power of the state and the instrumentalities of politics, just so long as they do not idolatrously pretend to be instruments of salvation, are "ordained of God" for proximate and limited but none the less vital ends. Justice is love operating at a distance, amid the impersonalities of the social and national communities; it is as Reinhold Niebuhr puts it "the alloy of love," giving to love the tensile strength to shift collective wrong; it does not represent that final transcendence of interest which is the fruit of grace and grace alone, but it does achieve that precarious balance of interests which makes human life livable this side of redemption; it is "the hard, general and rational skeleton of community indwelt by sin." It is a "dike against sin," by which men are shielded against the worst ravages of rampant pride and greed; but it is also a mechanism by which love can operate amid the collectivities of life.

To care for authentic justice is to do the work of love, and it is the nature of faith to be active in love. But precisely how are the final commitments of faith joined to the practicalities of politics? In this area also there is a large element of pragmatic calculation: "Absolute loyalties and pragmatic politics," in Niebuhr's useful formula. For political decisions are not to be derived simply from the data of revelation or the dicta of Scripture. Revelation clarifies the human situation in its ultimate dimension of love and responsibility to God and to neighbor, and the Scriptures illustrate how this final relationship of responsibility tutors the Covenant community at a particular time: but to transpose into the twentieth century the obligation of the Hebrew male to marry his brother's widow, or the Deuteronomic prohibition of usury, is to confine the care of the widow and of the poor in a time-bound frame which shuts it off from any living connection with the contemporary demands of the same compassionate justice. Political decision moves between the polarities of historic faith and contemporary fact: there is in every political decision an element of calculation because there is in every political decision an element of the technical. The demand of justice is perennial; the form of justice changes with the changing times. Faith and love do not dictate the technical decision; they enable it to be taken without prejudice. As a British friend of mine concerned with factory legislation is fond of saying: "We have to get from the Sermon on the Mount to dust extractors"—and this is quite a technical trick. We have also to get from the Sermon on the Mount to tariffs, FEPC legislation and the problems of private versus public power. At this point it is easy to become restive and to feel that the practicalities and technicalities are so complex that every decision is precarious, so precarious indeed that it becomes entirely hazardous. Many a group dedicated to social action has withered on the vine since the thirties—when the options seemed comparatively clear—because of an increasing and depressing sense on the part of many that we neither know with confidence what to do, nor have much hope that if we do what we think we ought it will have much impact upon the obscure and impersonal movement of events. This is one of the places at which the doctrine of justification meets us with peculiar reassurance. It will not let us kid ourselves that our decisions are less precarious than in fact they are, but it

can give a sanctity and urgency to the precarious choice which
no other stance save the stance of faith can provide. It delivers
both from the fanaticism of political dogmatism, and from the
freezing of political initiative which is less dangerous than
fanaticism but not more helpful. For it knows *ab initio* that
"the Almighty has His own purposes," which are never fully
comprehended by the minds of men, and never precisely accomplished by their contrivings: but more, it encourages us to
believe that the erroneous decision—the decision for example
on which we look back and say "I wish I had that choice to
make over again"—is not wasted if it is taken in faith, but is
built into a divine structure of activity that is wider than our
vision and wiser than our devising. Take, for example, the
vexed question of war and pacifism that once seemed so clear,
so clear indeed that in the early thirties pacifist opinion was
almost orthodox in American Protestantism. The fact that the
pacifist group has dwindled may well be due in part to a
softening of the Christian tissue, but it is certainly also due in
part to the increasing complexities of the time, which have
forced us to measure the human weight of war against a weight
of tyranny which many take to be worse than war. The fact
now is that Christian men of manifest and equal devotion go
their separate roads, some to accept the draft and some to
refuse it, each man if he is a man of sensitivity conscious that
given one new fact, or one new insight, the decision might
have gone the other way. The only consolation one can bring
at this point, where it is so tempting to resign responsibility
entirely, is that it is more important to be loyal than to be
right, that "the just shall live by their faithfulness" and not
by their good judgment, and that in the biblical reading of life

the Most High God may well use the work and witness of the faithful soldier and the faithful objector (who both have made their best choice and stayed with it) in a purpose wider than either can discern.

Yet while a right understanding of justification can sanctify the precarious decision no matter how precarious it is, the biblical faith does not leave us without resources for the sifting and sorting of alternatives. It gives us a relief map if not an ordnance map of the area of political obligation, and it has not a little light to throw on some characteristic contemporary questions.

One prime necessity, if the community of love is to be fruitfully related to the communities of law (and Christian love itself to political duty), is that they be rightly discriminated. For the Church has no parallel and few analogies among the communities of mankind. It is characteristic of the natural communities, the family and the nation for example, that they both nurture and fracture human community. The nation is both a nursery of solidarity and a symbol of division: and our Lord's ambivalent attitude to the family—his benediction upon it and his insistence that "in the kingdom of heaven they neither marry nor are given in marriage"—is a reminder that even this most precious of human groupings is grounded in an exclusiveness which makes it provisional and far from absolute. It is characteristic of human communities, also, that they live by antagonism. This is conspicuously true of the nation, which is most solid when it is most threatened; but it is true also of the family, whose legitimate interests can, like those of the nation, become the excuse for an enlarged and intensified selfishness.

It is fashionable in some types of Christian comment to compare the Church unfavorably with the disciplined efficiency of, say, the Communist Party. But the analogy does not hold at all: for the Communist Party in its aspect as a political instrument achieves political efficiency (where it does so!) precisely by the kind of discipline which the Church of its nature cannot employ. It can choose its members, which the Church cannot; and it can require a rigorous adherence to a "party line" which has no equivalent in the Community of Faith. For the Church is constituted not by political or any other kind of agreement, but by baptism and a simple confession of faith which represent the fact that what is being done in and through the Church is the re-establishment of the human community without restriction of political agreement, or temperamental affinity, or intellectual competence, or any other kind of coincidence whatsoever. The Church represents an undertaking paralleled nowhere else at all: the taking of ordinary human material and making a family out of it.

This unique *koinonia* is always perverted when it is turned into a political instrument; for the characteristic political questions involve technical judgments on which there is no ground for supposing that Christian men will agree. The characteristic political questions do not arise within the Christian community but in the human community. Political questions —concerning bread and freedom, education and sanitation— are human problems and not Christian problems; but just because they *are* human problems they are of endless and costly concern to Christian men. But as we work out our obligation in these typical political areas, there is no peculiar form of Christian duty, but only a peculiar Christian urgency to do our human duty well. There is no Christian definition of justice: it is humanly recognizable and humanly precious.[1] And Christian men will regularly find their allies, at the practical and political level, not on the basis of creedal affinity or community of faith, but among men who love justice and who can agree about what best serves justice in a present and particular case.

A recognition of the provisional character of all human societies serves two negative but vital ends: in the first place it is a safeguard against idolatry, for example of the nation; and in the second place it suggests what can and what can not be expected of the nation, which, like all human communities, is a community of interest. The same two distortions which we noticed earlier appear directly in connection with the nation: there are those Christians who sit indifferent to the problems of power because they think them a violation of charity; and there are those who waste good Christian breath exhorting the nation to eschew the politics of power, which is an aspiration precisely as hopeful as that a leopard should change his spots. A nation is a complex entity, difficult of definition: but there is no nation where there is no community of interest, and every nation is recognizably constituted of mutuality of interest, and organized to defend those interests against disorder from within and against threat from without. I happen to believe that President Truman's policies contained large elements of realism and good human sense; but his repeated assertion that

[1] It is regularly argued that there is no definition of justice at all, save possibly Aristotle's question-begging "to every man his due." As it is "humanly recognizable" it is close-tied to *equality*, and we would be prepared to argue that justice *is* equality, whether of opportunity, of possessions, or of rights before the law, except in those cases—which may well be very numerous—in which equality is a manifest violation of justice.

"American foreign policy is based on the Sermon on the Mount" was more amiable than accurate. And no access of piety in Washington will alter the hard fact that a nation's policies move always within the limits of a nation's interests. Christians are better employed asking how the nation's power can be used with restraint, and the nation's interests related to the common interest, than by calling on the nation for a transcendence of self-interest which is contrary to a nation's very constitution. What we may hopefully ask for, to refer directly to America's contemporary role in the world, is:

A. that the nation's policies take into account the degree to which this nation's interests are dependent on the common interest;

B. that our policy makers reckon with the long-term interests of the nation, and avoid panicky short-term judgments as to where those interests lie;

C. that our international procedures give rein to Christian and human altruism *within the limits* of the nation's interests. In view of the meager allotment for economic aid programs, there is much ground still to be gained under this head.

As over against the kind of spirituality which is either too delicate to have a hand in power-political maneuvers, or too idealistic about what can be achieved *by* such maneuvers, biblical faith would seem to imply a kind of wholesome secularism. It would recognize that not only are all politics power politics, but all sound politics are secular politics, bound within the circle (*saeculum*) of what is possible for man. A

Christianity, then, which can distinguish justification from justice and yet is concerned to relate them, would cherish what is possible at the political level, but would not be tempted to exaggerate it.

Let us see how such a "wholesome secularism" would operate in a number of crucial areas. To continue, for example, with a study of the nation within the community of nations. The recognition that the nation is a community of interest checks two contrary tendencies, common among Christians but not alone there: the first tends to be cynical about the elements of altruism in America's foreign dealing over these last years because, forsooth, the altruism is not unmixed; the second discounts the admixture of self-interest which infects all the nation's dealings, and makes too grandiose a claim. There have been elements of altruism in America's foreign policy, but not to the transcendence of interest. The first group disqualifies itself from any participation in policy making at all, since no measure of foreign aid could conceivably get through Congress unless it could be shown to be consistent with American interests: the second group in exaggerating American benevolence misjudges foreign reaction. For if we will notice that other nations are precisely as prone to self-justification as we are, it will not surprise us that the beneficiaries of America's bounty are sometimes less appreciative than we think that bounty merits. We shall understand further why America, with all her faults, is sometimes blamed for what is *not* her fault. The rich and the powerful of this world are, by the necessities of human nature, always a focus of resentment: for their riches mean that even their benefactions have the taint of patronage, and their power means that they must take a major share of blame for what goes wrong. These are the intransigent necessities of the human case, which can be lived with in the measure in which they are understood.

Still within the area of the role of the nation and its part in international life: the case for the United Nations should rest on the same modest and non-idealistic ground. Its positive achievements—in education, health and arbitration for example—are real enough if not spectacular. But even if they were non-existent, the main case for the UN would still stand. For it rests not on the ground of positive achievement, but on the necessity for the restraint of inordinate power. The American community, partly because of the biblical element in its inheritance, well understands this danger in its manifold domestic forms, and has both written safeguards into the Constitution, and structured them into the government. It should be possible to transpose and apply these same insights to the international scene. Even if the UN does not provide (as it probably ought not to provide) the structure of an international authority, it does provide a forum in which the policies of the powerful are put under scrutiny, and so under a minimum of democratic restraint.

The Christian case for democracy itself rests on the same practical and non-idealistic ground. It is not based on any notion that the voice of the people is the voice of God; but rather on the recognition that since no man's voice is the voice of God, no single human voice should have authority. And since the powerful are peculiarly prone to confuse their voice with God's voice, their interests with the common interest, it is directed to the restraint of inordinate power. It is based not on trust in the people so much as on distrust of the rulers. It is sordidly convinced that power is like money which is like dung—pestilential unless it be spread around. It affirms all men's worth and no man's wisdom. At this point biblical faith parts company with the "rational" politics of the Greeks. Greek rationalism provided no reality of democracy because it put too much store by man's wisdom and too little store by his worth apart from his wisdom. That is why the Greeks can dream of a philosopher-king, in whom power is conjoined with wisdom. This the Hebrews never do, knowing well that it is only in God that wisdom is securely joined to power, and that among men who are not God power cannot be joined to wisdom without corrupting the wisdom. They had a profound distrust of kingship, and when they did admit it, their prototype was not Solomon the wise, but David the Covenant man, who with all his unwisdom at least knew Whose servant he was.

For a politics without illusion, we have to take this recognition of the limited and provisional character of all political devices into all our political dealing. For all political associations are communities of interest. They are most powerful when the particular interest of the group coincides for the time being with the general interest,[2] so that men's egoism is yoked to their altruism, and they have the zestful sense that in serving their own cause they advance the common good. The Christian who takes a hand in the political game—and it is the present argument that all Christians are obligated so to do—must learn to find his way about among a tangle of con-

[2]As has the interest of industrial labor, by and large, over the last period. Labor in augmenting its own industrial power has created a more socially wholesome balance of power, and has therefore drawn the support, and rightly, of men who care for general justice. But that does not mean that the power of labor is not as susceptible of corruption, and as much in need of correction, as other kinds of power; as would shortly appear if the situation fell out of balance once again.

flicting interests, not only without being enmeshed in them, but
with an ability to manipulate the general good out of this very
tangle. There are available some useful working rules.

1. He must be ready to work for accessible ends by available means, to be content with modest gains and with no unmixed gains. There is a hearty normality about the main run
of Christian political work. The Christian is not after Christian
objectives: he is seeking wholesome human objectives with a
peculiar Christian energy. To return to a former example:
there is presumably no uniquely "Christian" way of organiz-
ing New York's water supply. There is a right way and many
wrong ways, and there are certain political devices by which
mistakes can be avoided and this particular good cause ad-
vanced.

2. Given that a Christian man accepts the modest possibilities of political action, there are certain "abnormal" qualities
which, provided he is prepared to learn the ropes and not to
jump them, he can bring to political life. He is not only prepared for hard and unrewarded work; but, since his political
work is grounded in love and not in resentment, it tends to
persist through those "between elections" doldrums when so
much political work languishes because the heat is off. He
does his work in a context of faith and understanding which
avoids fanaticism and therefore avoids disillusion. Aware of
the mixed quality of political motives, and the limited quality
of political gains, he is neither overexalted by provisional
success nor discomfited by present failure. Open-eyed about
the ambiguous character of all political groupings, including

the party of his loyalty, he will wage political war without bitterness though not without energy. All this generates a quality of critical loyalty which will increase his usefulness to the party of his choice, though not necessarily his immediate popularity within it.

3. A word ought to be said about the vexed question of "compromise" and the related matter of means and ends. There is a vast amount of Christian misunderstanding here. There are a great many Christians who would acknowledge in theory that political obligation belongs with the Gospel, yet shrink in practice from what they regard as the sordid necessities of political life, lest they become involved in a compromise of principle. Now it is meaningful to talk about a conflict of principle if life is being lived by principle: but we have already found reason to question whether Christianity provides a set of "principles" at all. It binds life in a matrix of obligation, which is a very different matter. To violate the obligation is of course a grave fault, but to pursue the obligation—for example the obligation to seek political justice—by every relevant means, is no compromise. We may flinch from the task or botch it—and to some extent we always do both— but there is no reason why we should not undertake it.

On the question of means and ends there is almost irremediable confusion (for which Aldous Huxley and the perennial philosophy must take some blame). It is doubtful in point of fact whether the Christian faith prescribes either means or ends. It sets tasks, political tasks among others. And if we must use the means-end formula in relation to political work, then we must say that in politics the end always does justify the means, provided the end is a good one, and provided we do not lose the end in the means. All actual political work is done on that basis: to protest otherwise is either cant or simple nonsense. Even the pacifists, who make much of this means-end formula, in point of fact simply calculate that the ends they cherish will not be served except by the means they choose.

4. The Christian recognition of the ambiguous and provisional character of all political work makes for a wariness of all "final" solutions of political questions. The price of political health, like the price of liberty itself, will be eternal vigilance. The perennial problem of church-state relations will serve as illustration here. For it *is* a perennial problem, for which no "final" solution is possible. For the Church is an anomaly in every state, and every state is a potential idolatrous threat to the Church. Church and state are good for each other as long as they are not at ease with each other. The mischief is in the "solutions," which either means that the State is subordinated to the Church, or the Church to the State. Even the "wall of separation" formula, we are beginning again to find, is provisional at best: for no judicial ruling can finally order the relations of two dynamic communities which interpenetrate each other at every point.

5. The events of our time are making it increasingly clear, and Christians in terms of their charter should be the first to see it, that the struggle for justice is best carried forward—and maybe can only be carried forward—by men who do justice. This hard but obvious necessity to do justice before we talk about it has been driven home especially to those who live

close up to the challenge of Communism, but it is implicit in the Faith itself. Here are *Lines to a Rickshaw Puller*, by a representative of Asian Christianity:

> *But now you shape your body*
> *to fit the wooden embrace*
> *of the hard sides of your rickshaw*
> *for its walls are your home, your rented home.*
>
> *I have seen you resentful and bitter*
> *when you spat on the ground*
> *and talked unconscious communism.*
>
> *I would like to put my hand on your shoulder*
> *and say to you, "Comrade,*
> *there is One who died for us*
> *and dying made us blood-brothers."*
>
> *But I am filled with the cowardice of the well-dressed—*
> . . . .
>
> *I am afraid you will wake with a start*
> *and betray resentment in your eyes*
> *as you see in me what I really am—*
> *your well-dressed enemy.*[3]

Justice belongs with justification, and justification illumines the urgency and the limitations of political justice. To be reconciled to God in Christ is not to be separated from our

[3]By Chandran Devanesan. Quoted by M. M. Thomas in *The Christian Scholar*, Autumn, 1954, p. 199.

human brethren, but to be so profoundly joined to them that their necessities becomes our intimate responsibility. Their prime necessities are bread and freedom, economic and political justice. To give men bread is not to affirm that they live by bread alone, but to witness that we do not.

To think well is to serve God in the interior court.

THOMAS TRAHERNE

Not only he who is in sin but he who is in doubt is justified by faith.

PAUL TILLICH *The Protestant Era*

6. *The Life of the Mind*

To reflect on the meaning of the life of faith is to raise the question of faith and knowledge. How do Christians know what they "know"; and how is what they know as Christians related to other things they know?

We have paid some attention already to the character of Christian faith as grounded in Revelation, and have suggested also the possibility of some new connections between such a faith and the deeper movements of the contemporary mind. On the one hand the Church has learned to speak of Revelation without embarrassment in the face of science and philosophy; on the other hand we find outside the Church an increasing recognition that the issues of life and of truth are not comprehended, still less exhausted, within the limits either of formal or of scientific logic. It is one of the anomalies of academic life in America that we have naturalistic and secular presuppositions structured into many of our academic disciplines at the very moment when those presuppositions are being influentially called in question, and the intellectual future is being shaped less by the scientists and more by the theologians and philosophers of existence. The "behavioral sciences" stand in clear and present danger of being trapped at this point.

On the other hand Christians have to watch their step too. No longer intimidated by a militant naturalism, their morale improved by the tempered claims of science and the resurgence of sophisticated and unsophisticated piety, they are tempted to claim science too easily as an ally, or to try to chase it summarily from the field. Both tendencies are to be discerned: the tendency on the one hand to say that because science cannot give us saving knowledge it cannot give us significant knowledge at all; and the tendency to suggest that science when you come down to it is just another kind of faith. The common form of this latter is the equation of the presuppositions of all scientific work—the accessibility and regularity of the external world and so on—with faith. Now it is important for the record to notice that scientific work rests upon scientifically undemonstrable presuppositions; but it has very little to do with the issues of faith. For faith in the biblical sense is not a presupposition: it is the response to grace and close kin to love. All the issues here are in need of an airing and are in process of getting it. Even the most modest contribution to the problem is worth offering, given that we can speak to the point.

By way of preliminary, we may mark certain hopeful signs on the frontier between faith and knowledge:

1. *The recovery of biblical authority without obscurantism.* Christian theology is learning after decades of conflict and adjustment to stand again on its own essential ground, which is the religious authority of Holy Scripture: and this without

any dependence on the untenable literalism which was an artificial defense against a destructive "modernism." The trouble with modernism was not its critical and scientific method of dealing with the biblical documents (that has yielded immeasurable gains) but its failure to take account of the character of the biblical documents as *canonical Scripture*. Of course the Bible is (a) a resource for the history of the ancient Near East, and for first-century Hellenism in some of its aspects, (b) a source book for religious ideas, though it is not so prolific here as might be expected, the Hebrews as we have seen not being given to speculation. But it is finally intelligible only as canonical Scripture, that is, as the record of the faith of a Community, and a chronicle of the events in which that faith is grounded. Even the structure of its parts is determined by the fact that in both Old Testament and New Testament you have a community of faith setting out the basis of the faith by which it lives. For the believing Community both Jewish and Christian what you have here is *Heilsgeschichte* (sacred history: history of salvation), that piece of history in which God peculiarly discloses His way and His will, that piece of history therefore which is the clue to all history. For the Jew it is "open" history whose fulfillment waits for the coming of the Messiah or the age of the Messiah; for the Christian it is both closed *and* open in a paradoxical way—its inner movement *disclosed* is Jesus Christ as the incarnate *Logos* (*logic* if you will) of life-and-history's meaning; its meaning still to be *realized* as the same Christ works His will and renders His judgment.

Earlier chapters at least suggested the uniqueness of the interpretation of life and history which stems from here. It

implies among other things a rejection of oversimple mean-
ings (rationalism and naturalism for example) and a conse-
quent vital and historical realism which plumbs the depths of
life in a way which neither speculative idealism nor scientific
naturalism has the power and range to do. This age-old mine
of insight is being opened up again, and the vein shows no
sign of being exhausted.

2. *The development of existentialism,* both inside and outside the Christian camp. The term is slippery: it is used here
very generally as a catchall for that whole trend of thought,
over the last 100 years, which includes thinkers as diverse as
Kierkegaard and Marx, Marcel the Roman Catholic and Sartre
the atheist. Its common element is the conviction that life is
more than either inductive or deductive logic; that the truth
of life yields itself rather to the integral will than to the detached, even dedicated, mind. Even where it is secular, it is
a kind of secular refraction of our Lord's saying that "The
pure in heart shall see God."

The presence and power of existentialist thinking prompts
some reflections about the Bible's own version of the way in
which truth is sought and found. For us children of the Enlightenment, thinking and believing are of the mind and for
the mind. But our congenial way of looking at the matter is
not the way of Hebrew-Christian faith. Quotations can readily
be multiplied:

Search me, O God, and know my heart; try me and know my
thoughts. (Psalm 139:23.)

Here *heart* and *thoughts* are not distinguished, but paralleled as in the typical Hebrew idiom. In other passages the heart is quite explicitly said to *think* and to *believe:*

> If you confess with your lips that Jesus is Lord and believe in your heart that God has raised him from the dead, you will be saved. For man believes with his heart. . . . (Romans 10:9.)

There is no point in trying to turn the men of the Bible into physiologists and psychologists; but there is something here which is not untypical of the biblical way of looking at life. In point of fact the Bible uses *heart* and *mind* interchangeably, suggesting that our choices are made at a level of life far deeper than mere ratiocination. "Create in me a clean heart . . ." (Psalm 51:10) might as well be translated "Create in me a clean mind . . ."; and conversely, "Be ye transformed by the renewing of your mind . . ." (Romans 12:2) refers quite clearly to the transformation or renovation of the heart or of the life. The "purity of heart" which Jesus makes the condition of knowledge of God equals singleness of mind, simplicity, essential integrity. In this respect biblical faith is closer kin to existentialism than to rationalism; it affirms that life is more than thought, that thought is always inextricably entangled with life, and that truth-for-life is to be found in decision and identification rather than in speculation.

We might notice here a somewhat negative point, that this ambiguity of the biblical language anticipates what we have come to call the power of *ideology*, the pressure upon our thinking of unacknowledged factors both psychic and social, so that our thinking is not so much preliminary to decision as it is a rationalization of decisions already taken under the pressure of passion or the concern about possession. We owe

somewhat to Freud, for example, the perception that our thinking is always under pressure from fear and hate and greed,
generated very largely from a predatory and frustrated sex.
We owe largely to Marx our recognition of the pressure of
interests, especially the interests of our economic class, and
our admission that in many matters of moment we think more
with our stomachs than with our minds. These have only
recently become commonplace; but they represent again empirical refractions of an insight of the Bible; which adds that
our thinking is entangled not only with our greed and passion,
but also with our pride. The first two distortions are part-
healed when they are known: the distortion of pride is healed
not when pride is recognized, but when it is overcome.

This issue thrusts still deeper. . . .

The habit of the intellectual is to bite off, intellectually,
more than he can chew—or choose; morally, to make, with the
mind, affirmations to which he is not committed with the will;
or to indulge, with the mind, in vast denials where, if the heart
really followed, life itself would become impossible. The
temptation of the intellectual, as John Baillie points out in
Our Knowledge of God, is to spin theories which we can believe as long as we live from the top of our minds, but which
reveal their fatuity as soon as we are touched in the bottom of
our hearts. We have already marked the salutary and clarify-
ing effect of exultation and of despair, the unreasonable yet
necessary quality of our commendation of compassion. A
dichotomy between heart and mind, between thought and life,
between theory and practice, can be a gap through which
streams all manner of hypocrisy and high-minded superfi-
ciality. That is one reason why the only safe place for the

theologian, for example, is in the thick of the social struggle: but the theologian is not the only intellectual who must save his soul alive.

So much for the preconditions of valid and saving knowledge. But what about intellectual knowledge—the knowledge of speculation and of observation—as such?

There has always been in the Christian tradition an ambivalence toward *learning*. The Bible itself commends *wisdom* (though it is wisdom in a peculiar sense, not unrelated to sophistication but by no means to be identified with it) but it also sets great store by what it calls *foolishness* (the foolishness of the Cross, the foolishness of preaching, and so on). We are to walk, St. Paul says, not as fools but as wise; yet the wisdom of this world is foolishness with God. Sometimes the paradox here is real and sometimes only apparent: the point however is that this play on words suggests some careful discrimination about what true wisdom is and what it is not.

Again, there is the same dialectic play between *innocence* and *maturity* (which presumably involves sophistication in some sense). To enter the kingdom a man must become as a child; yet once inside it, he must learn to put away childish things.

In the historic tradition the ambivalence takes on a structured form. Learning is sometimes cherished, sometimes abhorred and rejected. And in every structure the wholesome tension in the paradox tends to be lost: Francis of Assisi chooses to become as a little child; Calvin determinedly puts away childish things. Francis forbade his followers books, not only because he feared the pride of possession but because he feared the pride of sophistication; and his own successors as well as those of Calvin (of whom I am one) almost proved him right. Riches in the mind as well as riches in the bank can make difficult the needle's-eye entrance into the kingdom of God. Innocence and maturity somehow belong together in the life of faith, but humanly and historically speaking they are seldom found conjoined. Our Puritan fathers now nourished learning in universities which they called "encampments of the militia of Christ";[1] and now feared learning, partly because it threatened their own presuppositions and prerogatives, but also because of the wholesome insight that learning does threaten piety because it threatens humility.

What is the biblical truth of the matter, so far as we can now discern it?

1. The biblical summons to *righteousness* includes the summons to bring to God an obedient mind; an obedient mind, however, not a dormant mind. It is not without meaning that the Book of Job is in the canon, and that Job is commended for his intransigent determination to question all things in heaven and in earth, even the justice of God Himself. The service of the whole man which is the meaning of biblical holiness includes the service of the mind, as it does the service of all a man is and has. Sometimes the tradition will emphasize one aspect of the matter, as in Luther's doctrine of the sanctification of the manual crafts (see next chapter), and sometimes another—as in Traherne's "To think well is to serve God in the interior court."

[1] See *Excursus* by George Huntston Williams in *The Harvard Divinity School* (Boston, The Beacon Press, 1954), to which further reference will be made.

2. The meaning of our vocation to holiness is clear, in this matter as in others. But how to perform it, for men constituted as all men are? The mystery of evil touches the mind as it does the body: so that the obedient mind must be the transformed mind, as in St. Paul's "be ye transformed by the renewing of your mind, that ye may know. . . ." And in so far as in some sense we do our thinking with the heart or with the life, it is the renovated heart and life out of which is generated the valid service of the mind.

In the essay of George H. Williams already referred to, the distinguished church historian of Harvard describes the way in which this notion was wrought into the theological understanding of the university which informed the medieval world and came through Calvinism into the constitutive thought of our Puritan educationalists. It was conceived that by his primal disobedience Adam not only lost Paradise but with it the knowledge of the ways of wisdom, which are restored only in Christ:

> The *libido sciendi* and the *libido sentiendi* had together compassed the Fall of Man; and thus, in the monastic tradition of learned celibacy out of which the ideal of the medieval university in part developed, faith and continence were held to be the two ordained means of restoring reason to something of its paradisic perfection. . . .
>
> Even human as distinguished from divine knowledge (revelation) was thought to be most certainly secured from distortion and fragmentation through the dedication of the fellowship of learning to Christ the Truth as perceived from the vantage-point of the community of faith.

We shall return to this view of the community of learning; but the import of all this for our present purpose is that in view of

the desperate frailty of Adam and his descendants, which
means their capacity for self-deception, this side of the Fall
knowledge is only secure and undistorted when it is held under
the tutelage of faith, which is to say, of grace.

It is in this fashion that the Bible conjoins innocence and
maturity, humility and sophistication. Holiness is not the rejection of the mind and of its powers, but their godly use. But
in the measure in which, as we have seen, it is difficult to join
power to wisdom without destroying the wisdom, so is it difficult to join wisdom to humility without destroying the humility.
The conjunction of innocence and maturity is a signal gift of
grace.

3. The doctrine of justification by grace through faith is of
singular relevance to the life of the mind, and that in several
respects:

A. The Garden of Eden story warns us that the knowledge
of good and evil is forever withheld from men who are not
gods. And in our consideration of the moral life we saw how
perennially we have to act short of final certainty either about
motives or about consequences. But just as the knowledge of
final good and evil is withheld, so also is the final knowledge
of truth and error. In this sense among others faith is endemic
to life: "We have to decide prematurely in order that we may
act expeditiously," as Ralph Barton Perry says. In the Christian reading of life, however, we are not left without reassurance. For just as our precarious decisions are sustained and
fulfilled by a grace wiser than our wisdom, so our provisional
judgments made in faith are validated by a divine wisdom
which is one with the divine compassion.

B. The biblical and Gospel demand is for integrity and not accuracy. It is I think true to say that in the Gospels the only two sins to which damnation is inexorably joined are unbrotherliness and hypocrisy. It is the sin against brotherhood and the sin against truth which irrevocably shut man off from God. One might risk a comment in this sense about the mysterious "blasphemy against the Holy Ghost" which hath no forgiveness. A man may blaspheme against the Son of Man and be forgiven: which would seem to mean that a man may honestly reject Christ without wreaking destruction upon himself; but the sin against the Spirit of Truth . . . what can God Himself do with or for the man who will not acknowledge the truth he knows, or follow the light he sees?

"Have I the right to keep my faith," said a student inquirer, "at the price of my intellectual integrity?" The answer would have to be that the "faith" which is kept at such a price is no faith at all. The sin that damns is hypocrisy, not atheism, if we are reading the Bible aright. "The situation of doubt, even of doubt about God, need not separate us from God."[2] The really destructive atheism is not the denial of God; for that denial, if it is honest, keeps a man in the company of Job and other men of integrity. The really destructive atheism is fear of facts. For fear of facts, from whatever source they come— whether facts of biblical criticism, of physical science, of Marxist analysis—is the existential denial that the world is God's and that, as the Letter to the Colossians puts it, "all things cohere in Christ."

The doctrine of justification in the life of the mind would seem to mean that God can bring a man to himself by the way

[2]Paul Tillich, *The Protestant Era* (University of Chicago Press, 1948), p. xiv.

of honesty, even of honest doubt of God Himself; but that not even God Himself can bring a man home to Himself by the way of hypocrisy.

c. The necessity of free discussion, and of a free traffic in the sphere of ideas, is grounded also in the truth of justification by faith.

Free discussion has had its own liberal and somewhat romantic justification just as has the democratic idea. Milton's "Let truth and error grapple: who ever heard of truth being vanquished in a free and open encounter," is the equivalent in the sphere of ideas of the notion that the voice of the people is the voice of God: and it is just as vulnerable.

Free discussion does not ensure the emergence of truth, but it does check the idolatrous pretensions of error. It is the equivalent, in the sphere of ideas, of the democratic process in the sphere of political power.

More important still: the doctrine of justification by faith is the final validation of the contention which I think is William Blake's, that the mind of man should be "a thoroughfare for all thoughts, and not a select party." For just as we are not saved by right acts, so we are not saved by right thoughts (not even, incidentally, by right thoughts about the doctrine of justification by faith). And if we are not saved by right opinions then we need not fear wrong ones.

It is very important historically that where this aspect of the doctrine of justification is forgotten, a persecuting doctrine inevitably develops. Here we reluctantly take another Protestant cut at a Roman Catholic distortion. The Roman Catholic Church is much too solemn about overt denial, and overt atheism. We have seen how this betrays it into error in political matters; so also in the sphere of opinion. For in the context of a theology in which salvation has to be earned, it is easy to argue that part of the price is doctrinal conformity.[3] Of course it may be responded that Protestant history is far from clear of the same abuses, and that is true. But Protestantism falls into persecution only when it forgets its own constitutive principle, which is that salvation never can be earned, either by good works or right opinions. It is only the doctrine of justification by grace through faith which enables us to comprehend how God can pluck salvation out of the midst of every kind of error, even out of error about the doctrine of justification by grace itself.

All this has immediate pertinence to a question of pressing urgency, namely, the relation of the *community of faith* to the *community of learning*.

First a word or two about the terms in which the discussion is generally carried on, which seem to me compounded of confusion. The question is widely taken to be the relation of *religion* to *higher education*. Now there is clearly an issue here; or rather two issues, a constitutional issue and an issue of principle. The constitutional question has been trenchantly dealt with, for example, in Henry P. Van Dusen's *God in Education*,[4] where it is gravely questioned whether the "wall of separation" which the courts have taken to be implied in the First Amendment to the Constitution, was ever meant to be an iron curtain in the sphere of ideas. The issue of principle

[3]This is, of course, much too summary an account of Roman Catholic teaching; it refers to a trend and not to a formal definition.
[4]Charles Scribners Sons, New York, 1951.

is being forced upon our institutions of learning with increasing insistence. The present surge of popular piety, often indistinguishable from pure folk religion, the devout but highly ambiguous pressures from parents and alumni, and, more significantly, the discontent among students themselves that they should be religiously illiterate and in particular shamefacedly ignorant of their own religious inheritance—all these have already accomplished the augmentation of programs in the teaching of religion both in private universities and colleges, and in state schools.

It is at this point that the issue of principle begins to get confused. We have seen reason to discriminate biblical and Christian faith sharply from religion-in-general, and to point out that within the biblical world and outside it religion-in-general has been the prime and particular enemy of authentic biblical piety. But the Church itself is so infected with confusion here that it is almost impossible to keep the issues straight.

It seems to me clear that the schools—I am thinking especially of institutions of higher learning—have for constitutional and other reasons left undone much work that needs to be done in the sphere of religion. But how far is this a concern of the Church? No more and no less, it would seem to me, than would be similar neglect and inadequacy in the field of the physical or social sciences. If it is true, as I think it is, that the historical-social construct we call *religion*, in all its pervasiveness, influence and variety, has been subject to scholarly neglect, then the issue would seem to me to be one of scholarly responsibility, and not of Christian faith (except, that is to say, in so far as Christian men along with other men are concerned for the integrity and adequacy of all scholarly work). In point of fact tactical damage is done when the Church as Church presses for "more religion in education." For that simply raises the specter of Church encroachment, and rallies all the defenders, both pious and impious, of the "wall of separation." That the religious dimension of the life of man, both individual and corporate, should be examined with a scholarly diligence comparable with that given to its economic, geographic and psychological dimensions seems to me to be a question of academic respectability, in which the appeal should be to the conscience of the university as a scholarly community. It is a question in which the Church has no more vested interest than has any friend of sound learning: in point of fact the Church may have rather less, since the phenomenon of religion as the university should rightly treat it is Christian neither in bulk nor in meaning. But this is a point at which the Church should think rather of the health of the community of culture (just as in another connection we have seen that it should think first of the community of justice) rather than of its own polemical convenience.[5]

But no particular Christian interest is served by such a descriptive treatment of religion-in-general. So far we are at the periphery of the problem and not its core. For the Church holds with increasing articulateness a Faith which is the faith of a community and not a set of "religious ideas." It is an ingredient of the Western tradition (this is taken account of

---

[5]It is, incidentally, arguable whether religion should be treated, as so generally it is, in a special department established for the purpose. Not only is the relation of religion to culture pervasive rather than departmental, but it would appear that established departments—philosophy, psychology, history, sociology, art, for example—fall short of their scholarly duty if they do not treat the religious dimension of each separate discipline, and the religious elements germane to their field.

more or less adequately in courses in Western Civilization and the like), but stands also over against the Western and every other tradition, and on its own essential ground. The Faith, according to its own understanding of itself, is conjoined with the tradition yet does not derive from it. It validates the tradition's virtues while holding a criterion of judgment over its real faults and partial gains. Holding such a faith the Church must be related to the University—the Community of Faith to the Community of Culture—in some such way as it is related to the State: disparate yet conjoined.

The problem is not the communication of ideas at the intellectual level. That is simplicity itself compared with the real issue, which is to devise ways and means whereby the Community of Faith can be related to the Community of Learning (the Republic of Letters, in the traditional phrase) in such fashion that each is true to itself.

Now there are some obviously wrong ways to accomplish this. Mr. William Buckley, in his *God and Man at Yale*, affirms that the simple solution is that pious alumni should capture Boards of Tustees, fire all the atheists, and so make a free course for the Gospel (and for the teaching of laissez-faire economics, which he apparently believes to be part of the Gospel). This is strategically dangerous, since there is no guarantee that one fine day the atheists may not take charge of the Boards, and fire all the Christians; it is more than doubtful constitutionally; but more important, it denies the right of the University to be true to itself as a community of free and scholarly inquiry. For the University, like the mind of man, should be "a thoroughfare for all thoughts, and not a select party." The most that the Christian community should ask is that it be invited to the party.

The whole burden of our argument thus far implies that we should ask for nothing, in relation to the community of learning, which qualifies the character of that community as a community of free inquiry, in which nothing is required as a condition of citizenship in the republic of letters save the best service of the mind. We should ask for nothing, in particular, which threatens the real if relative autonomy of the scientific disciplines. They have suffered much at the hands of an obscurantist piety, which does not trust God enough to let the facts fall where they may. When the scientific disciplines won their freedom from the heteronomous tyranny of an obscurantist religion, they did the work of God. If they know their business they will keep that freedom against all the assaults of the pious: and from our point of view they should keep it, since there is no authentic piety to be won at the price of intellectual and scientific integrity.

To relate the Community of Faith to the Community of Learning in such fashion that each is true to itself: that raises all kinds of programmatic and structural questions which are beyond our scope here.[6] But the problem will clearly not be resolved unless it is rightly stated.

The question of the relation of Church and University is the corporate form of the question of faith and knowledge. George H. Williams—to revert to his momentous essay on the history of Harvard and its Divinity School—has reminded us that there is writ large in Christian history both medieval and Protestant the conception of Church, State and University as related to each other in a tripartite scheme in which the health

[6]Though we are not without some experimental light on them. The program, for example, with which the writer is associated at Stanford University, is conceived in these terms and has been so conducted for some useful years.

of each depends upon the autonomy and integrity of the others. In particular the Church in its more theologically alert periods has been eager to defend the integrity of the scholarly community not only as being established in the purpose of God, but as necessary for the health of the Church itself, whose tendency to inordinate pretension to doctrinal finality requires for its correction the uninhibited work and the rigorous scrutiny of a community committed to a truth unlimited by dogma. It may well be, says Williams in effect, that a contemporary Church tutored by the same faith may do a like service for the Republic of Letters, which has come again under threat.

Whatever be the contemporary need, however, it is clear that, in terms of our earlier discussion of humility and sophistication, Church and University need each other. Learning is greatly to be cherished, but there is no salvation in it. The condition of saving knowledge is simplicity and not sophistication. So both those of us who have no sophistication, and those of us who have enough to know there is no end to it, may take encouragement. Simplicity is at once harder and easier to come by than sophistication, but at least it is a quality in which the sophisticate has no advantage over the rest of us. He may even be at a disadvantage, in the measure of the store he sets by sophistication.

> *The trained mind outs the upright soul,*
> *As Jesus said the trained mind might,*
> *Being wiser than the sons of light.*
> *For trained men's minds are spread so thin,*
> *They let all kinds of darkness in,*

> *Whatever light men find they doubt it,*
> *They love not light but talk about it.*[7]

This is not to decry the life of the mind but to mark its dangers. The University needs the Church, for where else can be learned the meaning of the true *sacrificium intellectus,* which is not the abrogation of reason but its utter dedication in union with sincere feeling and a committed will? The Christian congregation has a final advantage over the scholarly community. For truth is not in detachment, but in immersion, in submersion, the submersion of the individual in the covenanted community which is sealed by Baptism and the Supper. To accept a community loyalty from which one cannot resile, to take with utmost seriousness the "homely ordinances" of bread and wine and water, which bind each to all and all to God: here is a way open to wise and to simple, which leads more surely to God than all the ways of the wise.

For this the life of the academic community can never substitute. But those of us who care for the University may permit ourselves to dream: that there may be conjoined with the Community of Learning a Community of Faith in which men being tutored in the simplicities may handle the complexities with integrity and fruitfulness; a community of men who, having learned simplicity, may bear sophistication with grace and without aridity.

The pursuit of learning is not the pursuit of salvation, but it is one of the fittest of occupations for the saved man. It is best conducted by those who know that there is no salvation in it.

[7]John Masefield. *The Everlasting Mercy.*

*The idea of duty in one's calling prowls about in
our lives like the ghost of dead religious beliefs.*

MAX WEBER *The Protestant Ethic*

7. *The Calling of a Christian Man*

It is the intention of this essay to show, without special
pleading if it may be, that the doctrine of justification by faith
touches every aspect of man's life, and touches nothing that it
does not illumine. From a discussion of ethics, politics and
culture we turn now to an area of concern—daily work and its
meaning—for which we have an inherited doctrine which was
developed in and from the Reformation in close conjunction
with the doctrine of justification by faith itself.

In Luther's conception the overcoming of self-love which
is the result of the ingression of the love of God transmutes all
human motives from concern for "our own advantage or salvation" to the pure and disinterested service of God. "What is
done is done just to please God thereby." This is the root from
which stems Luther's characteristic notion of the *calling*
(*Beruf*) of the Christian man. Christians are those who have
heard the word of the Gospel with such reassurance, and to
such destruction of self-love, that their "religious" anxiety
about their salvation is replaced by an overflowing love to God
who has accomplished that salvation by His work of love in
Jesus Christ. They are *called* to put away their anxiety and to
take their place with joy in the community of the justified, the
Church, which is constituted by God's *agape* and dedicated to

agape-obedience. By the call of God in the Gospel the Christian man is set in a new status (*Stand*). He is debtor to God for "all good things, and also salvation": he has received back his dignity as a son of God at the price of giving up his rebellion (that is, his self-love). His life henceforth is to grow from a new root of gratitude and filial obedience.

From this point Luther develops his characteristic and comprehensive doctrine of the calling (the vocation) of the Christian man. The man who acknowledges himself debtor to God is committed to serve him in the midst of the world. He accepts a new *Stand*—a new status of responsibility—in relation to other men. He is not only called into the community of God's debtors, but he is called to serve God in the total community of mankind. His *Beruf*, in fact, includes a number of *Stande*: that is, a number of specific responsibilities corresponding to his gifts and responsibilities—ultimately, in Luther's view, to God's appointment. He may be at once, a church official, a citizen, a cobbler and the father of a family. This matrix of obligation defines the form of his earthly vocation as it derives from his heavenly citizenship, his status as forgiven sinner.

More specifically, there are three areas of responsibility comprehended in every Christian vocation:

1. *The Christian as Churchman.* We shall be concerned directly with this in the final chapter. It is clear however that the Christian man's loving service of God will express itself first in his life as a loyal churchman, a member of the community of the justified. This is the heart of his calling; and the emphasis of Luther and the Reformation on this point implies

a high doctrine of the Church which is a world removed from the extremes of "Protestant individualism."

2. *The Christian as Citizen.* Commitment to the service of God binds a man also in responsibility for the necessary forms of social life: the family, the political community, the economic order of property and labor. The primal dignity which belonged to man before his rebellion involved "dominion over the earth": the restoration of that primal dignity restores also that high dominion, that delegated responsibility for the godly ordering of the created world. Love of God and the neighbor includes good citizenship, the care for the health of the body politic, and of all those forms of natural community upon which, by God's ordinance, the earthly well-being of man depends. The Christian man will perform the normal duties that fall to all men as members of the natural communities, but he will perform them with a peculiar and particular diligence, in the measure of his love for the brethren for whom Christ died. "We ought freely to help our neighbor with our body and its works, that we may be 'Christs one of another.' " Vocation is the *Werkhaus* of neighborly love.

3. *The Particular Calling of the Particular Man.* Within the general area of citizenship obligations, which fall equally upon all men and with peculiar urgency upon all Christians, each man is to distinguish a particular calling appointed for himself, that piece of the world's work which falls only to him; by faithful performance of which he is to honor God, serve the neighbor in a unique fashion, and keep himself in the godly trim of disciplined Christian living.

It is Luther's doctrine of the particular calling, transmitted through Calvin and Puritanism, which still informs the churches of the Reformation in so far as they are true to themselves. But his simple formulation has been overlaid by all kinds of historical complications, and obscured by all kinds of modern and self-justifying devices, so that its capacity to illumine our contemporary problem can by no means be taken for granted.

What Luther did was to separate the work of the world irrevocably from the work of salvation, which of course is not a work at all, or rather, is a work of God and not a work of man. He believed that the medieval Church had fallen away from the primal Christian confidence in Christ's finished work on man's behalf, and fallen back into an anxious concern about salvation, refusing "to take God at His word." This meant in historic practice an undue priority for the cloister, and those occupations which appeared to minister more directly to man's spirituality, his approach to God along the road of self-purgation and ascetic piety. But Luther—and here he would appear to have the Bible behind him—was less interested in spirituality than in the plain and practical service of God. The spiritual piety which is the fruit of religious anxiety is for him the type of unfaith. The man who believes *has* his salvation— *Wer glaubt, her hat*—and will shift all his concern from salvation to service. And the service of God, to take the argument one stage further, is the service of the neighbor, not in terms of *our* spiritual progress, but in terms of *his* plain and practical necessities.

The symbol of this shift is that in his translation of the Bible

Luther takes the word *calling* (in Greek *klesis,* in German *Beruf*), which had previously been reserved for the more spiritual occupations, and uses it where previous translators had written simply *Werk* (work). The effect of the shift, in the developing thought of the Lutheran Reformation, is to give to the ordinary run of human work the Christian dignity that had traditionally belonged to the cloister and the clergy. Now here he is affirming nothing that had ever been formally denied; but what is new in Luther, and momentous for Christian history, is the passion and the power with which he glorifies the secular life, and the consistency with which he affirms that the test of a true Christian vocation is not spirituality but social utility. To the magistrate, the farmer, the soldier, the artisan, the servant girl, he cries that God has given them their station, that if they take it as appointed by God it is "a status higher than that of a bishop." "The common status of a Christian is the holiest on earth." And it is holy not because it ministers to salvation, but because it ministers to the common good.

This sanctification of the common life was and is substantially valid in the light of the biblical version of holiness, and it directly belongs to Luther's reaffirmation of the New Testament doctrine of justification. It was effective also for Luther's objective of destroying the "double standard" which gave undue priority to the cloister. But it became a principle of social conservatism for two reasons at least.

1. Luther unjustifiably extends the meaning of the biblical *klesis,* when he suggests that a man is *called* to be a farmer or

a soldier or a servant in the same sense and almost in the same act as he is called to be a Christian.[1]

The fundamental meaning of the call of God is that man is uprooted from the circle of his self-idolatry and set in a new relation to God and his fellows.

> In the New Testament *vocation* means God's call to repentance and faith and to a life of fellowship and service in the Church. The Bible knows no instance of a man's being called to an earthly profession or trade by God. St Paul, for example, is called to be an apostle; he is not "called" to be a tent-maker.[2]

Of course a man comes to God as he is with all that he has, including his powers of hand and brain—this is the strength and relevance of what Luther has to say—but to say that a man is appointed to be a servant by the same act in which he is appointed to salvation is to sanctify the common life in too unqualified a fashion.

2. The effect of Luther's teaching was to root the hierarchical structure of feudal society directly in the will of God, so that every relationship of dominance and subordination was equated with the divine will. The same doctrine was later utilized to harden Puritan patriarchalism into a pattern of tyranny which for the sake of elemental justice had to be shattered by the industrial revolt.

The fact is that Luther was a medievalist in social understanding. He took it for granted that the hierarchical ordering

[1] There is a most careful and illuminating analysis of the biblical doctrine of vocation in Alan Richardson, *The Biblical Doctrine of Work* (S.C.M. Press, London, 1952).

[2] Richardson, op. cit., p. 35.

of life was wholesome in itself, that the varieties of work and responsibility which it allotted were each worth doing, and meshed in a pattern of social well-being. In other words his test of social utility as defining what is "wholesome work for a Christian" was used conservatively and not critically. The truth and the limitations of his doctrine have since been clearly seen.

In our contemporary day it becomes vital to notice both the truth and the limitations of the doctrine. For we have another situation in which the work of the world has fallen into disorder. Our problem is not the double standard as between the cloister and the common life. But our estimate of the way in which work should be chosen and work should be done is subject to a new set of confusions, which can be clarified only if we recover the essential truth of Luther's affirmation, rid of its limitations.

The limitations of the doctrine became clear as soon as the heirarchical society was disturbed by historic change, and called in question by a new impulse of justice. The Puritan version of the vocation doctrine, which was essentially Luther's at least into the early part of the seventeenth century, was relevant and illuminating for the life of the patriarchal household. For in that typical Puritan establishment the family and the immediate employees constituted a little kingdom. The function of the head of the household was to rule that kingdom well; the servant had his own status and his own calling, but his status was one of subservience, and his calling was construed as hard work and docility. In the authoritative teaching of William Ames:

[Masters] ought to bear themselves towards their servants with humility, and meekness, not imperiously, and domineering.

. . . [They ought, however, to] correct saucy servants (Proverbs 29:19) or if they be incorrigible, to turne them out of dores (Psalm 101:6).

Servants, for their part,

. . . owe to their Masters subjection as well as honor . . . they ought to obey their Masters in the Lord, in all things, wherein they are subject. . . .

The pattern was tolerable to the worker as long as the form of the patriarchal society was secure; for within it the worker was guaranteed a meaningful status, and, on condition of docility, a minimum security. It became intolerable as soon as the pattern of the patriarchal society was broken up, and a nascent industrialism wrenched the workers out of the patriarchal household and put them to work at the machines, machines whose authority was to become as absolute as that of the old Puritan proprietors, and a good deal less considerate. Never at any stage during the painful and exhilarating history of industrialism has the inherited doctrine been translated in such a way as to illuminate the new status of the worker or, for that matter, of the industrial proprietor and his professional affiliates. In American Protestantism the doctrine survives for the proprietors in an emasculated form as a doctrine of stewardship and benevolence: for the worker it survives in the form of an outworn ethic of docility—"a good day's work for a good day's pay"—which is to say that it scarcely survives at all.

The new self-consciousness of the Church, its concern about its long tradition and its present relevance, has generated a new surge of interest in the vocation problem among others. But the effort at retranslation of the inherited doctrine has been impeded by at least three deep-driven prejudices:

1. Greek rationalism has infected the minds of many who have never heard of it. It comes in part transmitted through the Christian tradition, which bears much unbiblical lumber along with the authentic Word and Sacraments. Of course any generalization about Greek thought is of necessity too simple. But the effect of the rationalistic strain in the tradition is to give an undue priority to intellectual over manual skills. Many a member of the American community, who boasts that his ancestors cleared the wilderness with their own hands, or manhandled ox wagons across prairie and mountain, will spend endless pains to save his children any risk of being involved in such work, at least for a living, and will torture and strain his bank balance and the minds of his offspring to win for them an entree into the professional and intellectual class. The professional and humanities schools of our universities are partly peopled by youngsters whose real predilections and personal gifts would make them first-rate tractor drivers or short-order cooks, but whose actual vocational choice is neither practically nor biblically justified.

2. In so far as our common mind is shaped by the Puritans rather than by the Greeks, the effect is to give a priority not so much to the intellectual occupations purely as such, but to the responsibilities of ownership and management, the characteristic occupations of the old middle-class, which stands under most direct tutelage of the Puritan fathers.

Both of these prejudices take too little account of the social utility, and therefore of the Christian significance, of the run of the world's work, which is neither intellectual nor managerial.

3. Both of these prejudices are curiously mixed with and subtly reinforced by a type of spirituality which fails to take account of the radical reassessment of the whole religious issue which we have seen to be involved in the biblical revelation. Not even the Christians have been able to believe with their whole heart that, as Luther put it once for all, "God has taken care of my salvation." There is always an intrusive anxiety to measure our status with God by the quality—or rather by the quantity—of our spirituality. The effect of this upon vocational choice is an undue priority given to "professional Christianity," specifically to the ministry and related occupations.

The temptation here is peculiarly subtle. There is not only the feeling that professional religious work has a more direct Christian significance than the ambiguous procedures of industry and commerce, but also the sense that a day-by-day and all-day preoccupation with spiritual matters will facilitate and enhance the quality of one's own spiritual growth. Add to this the fact that we are far removed from the days of the apostles, and that the professional ministry also carries with it the aura of middle-class professionalism, with its social spaciousness and relative security, and you have a multiple distortion of the Christian perspective on the whole matter. The present overcrowding of theological seminaries is not, probably, to be deplored. But it raises the question whether those who offer themselves for "full-time Christian service" have in every case measured their particular gifts with precision and related them in terms of social utility to the plain needs of men. On

any reading of the biblical faith and the Reformation inheritance God is better served by a qualified mechanic than by an
unqualified cleric.

There is, of course, no point in stationing oneself at the
door of the seminary to turn good mechanics back into industrial life in the name of the Lord and of Luther, unless we can
help them to see with some kind of clarity how they can keep
a Christian course there.

First, and positively, the reiteration of the biblical and
Reformation doctrine ought to bring profound resource and
invigoration to the laity. The pious perversions to which we
have referred have been a cause of real frustration both to the
clergy, in their concern to find "Christian work" for the laity;
and to the laity themselves, who have so often either had to
persuade themselves that they were gifted for choir-singing or
Sunday-school teaching, or have had to cabin and confine their
authentic Christian motivation within the limits of ecclesiastical trivia and church organization. Now there is a sense
in which nothing is trivial which affects even the organizational
health of the people of God: but the real Christian "front of
struggle" (to borrow a Communist phrase) is not within the
very necessary church organization, but in the very places
where non-professional Christians live, and where the clergy
cannot effectively enter—the secular professional association,
the labor union, the learned society and the League of Women
Voters. It is not only that the work there represented—the
daily work of production and distribution, of construction and
teaching and of local body politics—is itself work of high

dignity on any Christian reading of the matter; it is also that in these areas are shaped the day-do-day decisions which tell for or against freedom, justice and good social order. We have simply not learned, in the contemporary church, to magnify the work of the laity in its own terms and for its own sake. Nor have we learned how to draw the laity into the councils of the church in such fashion that the common Christian mind may be enlivened and enriched by insights which are quite beyond clerical competence.

While there are large areas of high responsibility where the non-clerical Christian is fully on his own, and will have small help from the professionals, none the less there is an abundance of strictly theological work to be done in translating the inherited vocation doctrine in such fashion that it makes illuminating connection with the facts of contemporary and secular life. At the moment the connection is not clear at all. Let me list one or two examples picked quite haphazardly.

The pious distortions of the doctrine which I have enumerated appear with regularity in student discussions of the Christian faith and life. In my itinerating among the American colleges I visited a southern university of considerable influence and with a strong Christian inheritance. As is customary on such missions, I was invited to visit a number of classes and to try to suggest some connection between the Christian faith and the particular discipline which was the subject of the course. I had been in philosophy, in education and so on. One morning my student guide arrived in a high state of merriment. "I can't imagine," said she, "what you're going to say to them this morning." I inquired what the problem was and why life was so funny. "Why," she said, "we're visiting a class of sanitation engineers!" No problem about philosophy, and none with education, apparently, for both of these presumably have elements of rationality and sophistication highly congenial to a Christian theologian: but sanitation engineers! Now in point of fact the connection between Christianity and sanitation is a good deal clearer than the relation between Christianity and philosophy. If the test of the validity of a theoretical or practical discipline is its plain social utility, then the social utility of sanitation is a good deal clearer than the social utility of philosophy. And if the community had to choose between doing without its sanitation engineers and doing without its philosophers, the choice, to put it mildly, would not be obvious.

Again, how often one's heart sinks to be told, in conversations with students about their vocational choice, that what they want above all things is, as they put it, "to work with people." The tone is always pious and the intention admirable: but what in fact is meant is that they have no intention of any kind of manual craft, and that their work with people is to be on the professional level—professional social work, or personnel work, or YWCA work, or something of the kind. Now there is nothing mischievous about any of these. The mischief is in the assumption that they are more elevating than manual work, and that they bring you close to people, which they do not. The profoundest relations of life are not accomplished across a counselor's table, but in the comradeship generated out of doing a common job of work. It is the recognition of precisely this which has created the worker-priest movement of French Roman Catholicism, and related movements in a number of Christian communions. To enter a "secular" profession or to work at a factory bench is not to be cut off from people; it is in a sense to join the human race.

This positive point made, however, we are still far from the nub of the contemporary problem. For there is a great bulk of contemporary work to which it is very difficult to attach the dignity of work done to the glory of God and for the common good. As to whether there is more ambiguity attaching to contemporary toil than to the work of previous generations of men is, as the sage Guillim said of a certain question in heraldry, "a question of more difficulty to be resolved, than commodious if it were known." In any event the fact of ambiguity is there, and it is quite extraordinarily difficult for many men of Christian intention to see how the work on which their livelihood depends can be construed in Christian terms at all. Sometimes the difficulty arises from an excessive spirituality related to the distortions we have described. There is a good deal of finickiness. I came on a Christian congregation in these United States which was much disturbed and perplexed because a man had applied for membership who was a waiter in a night club. The first comment on their dilemma would seem to be that if there is one social group too sparsely represented in the Church it is waiters in night clubs.

But very often the dilemma lies deeper. We are on delicate ground here: but how much of the vast apparatus of competitive selling, which enlists so many of our people and such a bulk of literary and artistic talent, is in any direct fashion related to the social good? It can be justified in all kinds of oblique ways, and, for all the wasteful elements in it, no doubt it does in its bizarre and roundabout fashion put life insurance and washing-machines more or less where they are needed; but the vast apparatus of ingenuity devoted to demonstrating that cigarette A is milder than cigarette B, when producer, advertiser and consumer are perfectly aware both before and after the operation that cigarette A is precisely as mild as cigarette B—this is an example of the kind of ambiguity which takes the lilt out of any high and moving utterance about Christian vocation. For no matter how we reassure ourselves by legitimizing the work in terms of the presuppositions of modern commercialism, it still lacks urgency when measured by any high and valid standard of what constitutes the human and social good. It is a very moving thing to discover how spontaneously a group of churchmen up to their ears in commerce will respond to any suggestion that their dilemma is even understood. For the most part it goes unacknowledged, but it creates a profound unease: especially when the clergy either do not refer to it at all, or, equally unhelpfully, simply throw a pious sanction over the whole commercial and industrial melee.

At this point Luther's statement of the vocation doctrine is only of limited usefulness. We are eternally indebted to him for his re-establishment of the doctrine of justification as the fount of all valid piety. It is from the same starting point that we shall have to spell out a relevant contemporary formulation. But the doctrine will have to be more *critical* than it was in Luther's statement. Because he took for granted the validity and social utility of all the forms of work characteristic of his day,[3] he dealt with the problem of daily work as a problem

[3]With the one exception of banking, which is mildly ironic in view of the affinity of modern Protestantism with the financial and commercial classes. Luther explicitly included the hangman as exercising a tolerable Christian vocation, but he could not stomach the Fuggers. Of course the modern banker is not the late-medieval usurer.

affecting simply the relation between a man and his appointed job. To perform a Christian vocation, in Luther's understanding of the matter, was simply to do the given job well.

This will not do for our day. For on any given job, that man who does it is involved in a mesh of obligations which include not only his obligation to the work itself and to his employer if he has one, but to the members of his trade union or professional association, and to the consumer public to whom the given product or service is eventually offered. Not only so, but the conditions under which production and distribution are carried on—the conditions for example under which oil is tapped and marketed, or the conditions under which the American and Swiss watch industries are related to each other—are questions of general social importance, affecting not only the immediate constituency of producers and consumers, but the stability and equity of the whole political-economic society. To take Christian vocation seriously, in any relevant contemporary terms, involves not only the diligent performance of the work that lies to hand, but the informed and incisive criticism of the conditions under which the work is done. Of course the latter is ineffectual without the former. A doctor may have grave questions about the social vision of the AMA, but his utility as a constructive critic of AMA policies is pretty precisely related to his professional competence.

In some such terms as these we may look for the development and application of the inherited doctrine. But if it is developed more critically it must also be developed more *politically*. For a great many of the issues which arise when the form of the world's work are put under scrutiny are political questions. It was the development of new forms of industrial property, and the patterns of work related to them, which negated the Reformation formulae as they come from Luther through Calvin and the Puritans. A rigorous concern to develop an understanding of what Christian vocation means in the twentieth century will involve an equally rigorous attention to the work- and property-patterns characteristic of our society. For these patterns may either lend recognizable dignity to the work of men's hands and minds, or destroy the possibility of finding any dignity there at all.

The Church of God is born of God's Word, abides therein, and knows not the voice of a stranger.

JOHN KNOX

This Catholic Church hath been sometimes more, sometimes less, visible.

The Westminster Confession of Faith (1648)

8. The Integrity of the Church

Daniel Jenkins is writing good sense at some length about the Church in another volume for this series.[1] But there is no way in which we can gather together the various concerns which occupy the bulk of this essay except by a discussion of the Church: for the Church is the Community of the Justified; Christian ethics are the *ethos* of the *koinonia* (the Church fellowship); the problem of politics is the relation of the community of faith to the community of law; the problem of faith and knowledge is, in concrete terms, the problem of the Church and secular culture; and the calling of a Christian man is first the call to take his place in the Church, and then to let his public life be governed by the faith that is generated and nurtured *there*.

Extra ecclesiam nulla salus (outside the Church there is no

[1] He is also the author of *The Nature of Catholicity, The Gift of Ministry* and *Tradition and the Spirit* (all published by Faber and Faber of London). The last has been republished in this country as *Tradition, Freedom and the Spirit* (Philadelphia, The Westminster Press, 1952). They constitute together the most sustained and important discussion of the Church and its Ministry to be produced, at least in English, in our day.

salvation) is a biblically-grounded and thoroughly Protestant principle. It simply seals and symbolizes the consistent biblical testimony that the purpose of Christ's death was "that he might gather into one the children of God." To be damned is to be lost (*damnos*) in the isolation of self-idolatry: to be justified (*justus*) is to have this sorry condition rectified, and to be knit within the body of the new humanity. The very act of baptism represents the death of the self: and the new self which rises from the water of baptism is a self rid of the self-isolation which is damnation. We rise with Christ, but with Christ as the first-born of many brethren, the Elder Brother of the reconstituted family of mankind. Individualistic Christianity is a simple contradiction in terms. Biblical religion is not, in Matthew Arnold's phrase, "what a man does with his solitariness": it is a way of deliverance from the death of solitariness to the life of solidarity with the brethren for whom Christ died. Of course this does not mean that the limits of the church organization coincide with the frontiers of the Church and Kingdom of God: but it does mean that we cannot draw near to God by drawing apart from our fellows, but only by accepting them as the kinsmen they are. The Church, then, is not a device for individual spiritual nurture, nor for advancing the Christian cause in the world: it is, in so far as it is true to itself, an end in itself, the very fruit and meaning of Christ's death.

"True to itself . . . ," "an end in itself . . ."—these can easily be misleading. For the Church is not its own master—"One is your Master, even Christ": so for the Church to be true to itself is to be true to its Lord, of Whose death it is born and by Whose life it is nourished. And if it is true to Christ it will not live unto itself. Nevertheless, over against every kind of individualism it must still be insisted that in so far as the Church is the reconstituted family of mankind, it does not exist first of all as an instrument for Christ's work, but as the fruit of it.

It is in this sense that the spokesmen of the ecumenical movement, that massive movement of church reformation, have always said, somewhat enigmatically but none the less truly, that the first business of the Church is to be itself: "Let the Church be the Church." In the words of W. A. Visser 't Hooft, "The task of the Christian now as always is to prove that the Church exists." He means, I take it, that the best service the Church can render to the sundered communities of mankind is to demonstrate in its own corporate life that the broken family is in process of being knit up again, so that divisions within that family have become both anachronistic and blasphemous, a denial to the Lord Christ of the fruit of His soul's travail.

This is the high doctrine of the Church by which all the churches of the Reformation are governed, in continuity with the great tradition. It is written deep in their Confessions: and the extract from the Westminster Confession which prefaces this chapter would suggest that it is the business of the Church to let the reality of a reconstituted humanity be visible in its own life, and to be constantly wary lest the reality of the new humanity be obscured by church abuses, either of disunity, apostasy or idolatry.

The prime concern of the Church, then, is with its own integrity, with the consistency of its life as the community of the justified, the reconstituted body of mankind, the household of faith. But what does this corporate life of faith involve? We

may begin by taking account of the character and meaning of
the individual act of faith.

What is faith? Colloquially speaking, almost anything
under the sun. *Faith* is a blanket term which covers (A) belief in something you know isn't true (schoolboy definition);
(B) the conviction that if you square the hypotenuse of a right-
angled triangle it will equal the sum of the squares on the other
two sides; (C) faith in So-and-So's toothpaste or breakfast
cereal or in grandma's recipe for Christmas pudding; (D)
faith that the barber won't cut your throat under pretense of
shaving you; (E) faith in President Eisenhower's leadership
—or in President Truman's; (F) faith in democracy or the
United Nations; (G) faith in God (whoever he may be); (H)
Christian faith (whatever that may be).

This is only moderately helpful. Faith has obviously got
something to do with trust or confidence, but that is about as
far as the colloquial use takes you. And you don't narrow it
down much if you talk about religious faith or even faith in
God. There is the story of an English M.P. who, after the 1928
debate in the Commons on the Revised Prayer-Book, came out
of the House muttering that he didn't see what all the fuss was
about. "Surely," said he, "we all believe in some kind of a
something." The content of the act of faith would seem to be
defined by "what kind of a something" we believe in.

Faith is defined by its object: and the object of Christian
faith is Jesus Christ as the Scriptures testify of Him. So we
understand what Christian faith is in proportion as we understand who Christ is. But there is another term in the correlation. What about the Christian man, the man who "has" this
faith? For faith would appear to be determined not only by its

object but by its subject, by *how much of the man* goes into the act of faith. Faith that "the square of the hypotenuse of a right-angled triangle equals the sum of the squares on the other two sides" is a conviction of the *mind* related to mathematical consistency; faith in grandma's recipe may be an affair of the *heart*, based on clan loyalty rather than on a rigorous care for truth; faith in democracy or the United Nations enlists the *will* to make them work. So faith may be intellectual, an affair of the mind; or it may spring from the heart as a kind of personal loyalty; or it may be an affair of the will, a kind of moral commitment and determination.

Luther, as we saw, strips the act of faith *bare*. It partakes, he says, of the nature neither of love nor of obedience, for how can there be true love or true obedience this side of the act of justification, in which the self abdicates that Christ may reign? A man must take his salvation before he can live like a saved man. And in some sense this is true: yet even Luther I think would agree that when God lays hold of a man it is the whole man that He lays hold on; and that therefore Brunner is right to say that "Faith is a totality-act of the whole personality." It is the act of the whole man. Now what a "whole man" is it is not easy to say, and until we do know what a whole man is we shall have to do without a complete definition of faith. But we know that man is compound, to speak still colloquially, of heart and mind and will, so that the act of faith involves at least these three, close-joined as they are in the biblical understanding of man. The life of faith is like driving a three-horse chariot (or rather letting it be driven) in the race that is set before us, and you get a distorted Christian life—something less than a full life of faith—if the horses don't run evenly in harness. If heart and will lag behind the mind you get a barren Christian intellectualism without heart or guts; if the heart gets out of hand you have emotionalism run riot; and if the moral sense is isolated from thought or feeling you get the kind of faith which will give its body to be burned, yet is nothing because it lacks love. Of course our response to Christ is never total: each one of us is slanted—to intellectualism, to emotionalism, or to moralism. That is one reason why we need the nurture of the Gospel and the Church.

There is somewhat the same triple and total character to the corporate life of the Church. The Church is called to serve God with the integral mind, the loyal heart, the obedient will. Its triple service is represented in corporate practice by the concern for valid worship, for sound (which is to say salutary) doctrine, and for a discipline of life which is shaped by the obedience under what the Church stands. The problem of the Church's integrity is oversimplified if we forget the triple character of its corporate life of faith: for the Church is subject to the same temptation as is the individual to fall into sentimentalism, intellectualism or moralism. It is tempting to think that there must be a single formula for the healing of our present distempers, and we are tempted to make the recipe according to our taste and prejudice. The people who like a rarefied intellectual air tend to tell us that "all our problems are at bottom theological," that our trouble is the incoherence of contemporary preaching and the confusion that has reigned in the sphere of doctrine. We are accumulating a mass of valid and critical theological work. I have read seminary papers which were packed with the dynamite of church revolution— were they not simply seminary papers.

We are not long out of the meeting of the theological reformers when we are called to another, this time to be told that the Church's trouble is the lack of a relevant social message. The need is not so much the recovery of a dogmatic tradition as the development of a relevant and contemporary social critique, and a program of political and economic reconstruction which will outmatch Communism on its own essential ground. The speaker at *this* meeting has scarcely ended when someone rises at the back of the hall to give it as his (or her) view that we have had enough of barren theorizing and large-scale programs of social change: our problems will be solved only when we recognize that our real need is a deeper devotional life, in which we return to the interior roots of illumination and of power.

This is partly caricature. Our doctrinal, social and liturgical thinking at its best is much better than this. But it will serve to emphasize that as the individual life of faith is a total life, so the corporate life of faith is a totality-act of the Church as a whole, in doctrine (which is the loyalty of the mind), in liturgy and the life of prayer (which is the offering of the heart's love) and in discipline (which is simply discipleship: the conformity of the will to the Divine will). Lose any of these or pull them apart from each other and you get radical distortion in the life of the Church—a barren dogmatism, a false pietism or a bare and soulless ethic.

The Church which is to meet and minister to men at the end of their human tether will have to hold its total life under the Word by which it is constituted a Church, it will have to submit to perennial reformation in worship, doctrine and discipline. For its worship must make explicit the reality of the new humanity, its doctrine must make divine sense of a world which makes no human sense at all, and its discipline must give shape and body to the profound solidarity which is generated out of the recognition that we are all the younger brethren of Christ.

What has to be said here can be most simply said if we utilize a characteristic New Testament symbol for the Church —*the household of faith,* or *the household of God.* The figure of the family is homely enough for any purpose, and comprehensive enough for ours. And the analogies which it offers with the community of faith are many and illuminating.

1. In the first place, there is no family without its *pedigree,* no Church without its fathers in the faith. The community of faith is united not in the first place by agreement in the sphere of ideas, but by a common ancestry. The community of faith is the community which takes as its own God the God of Moses and of the prophets, and is content that its common life be governed by His Word. To become a Christian is to become a Jew, and to be a Jew is not to be an ethical monotheist (whatever that may mean) but to be one with Abraham, Isaac and Jacob in the community that God has chosen to be His people in the midst of the world.

> Jewish history is, in essence, *Heilsgeschichte,* redemptive history. But it is not merely the history of redemption, it is the history which redeems. Only by appropriating, in faith, this history as his own, by making it, so to speak, one's own past, does the Jew become a believing Jew.
>
> "All this I do," the Passover Haggadah represents the Jew as saying, ". . . because of what God did for *me* by bringing me forth from Egypt."[2]

[2] Will Herberg, "What Is Jewish Religion?" *Jewish Frontier,* October, 1950.

And as for the Jew so, *a fortiori*, for the Christian. For the same redemptive history, as the Christians understand it, comes to its crown and climax in the venturesome holiness and the saving accomplishment of the Covenant-man, by Whom God "brings many sons unto glory." To be a Christian is not to agree with other Christians about a set of religious ideas, but to acknowledge that the work Christ did—in illumining this world's darkness, breaking the deadly circle of the self and taking the sting out of death—was done for us. The thing is concrete, historical, corporate—if you like, ancestral.

2. Then again, on the analogy of the human family, the Church with its pedigree inherits a store of *family lore*, and develops through the generations its own *ethos*, which is what we actually mean by "Christian ethics."

In the sphere of truth, first of all: just as we know what we know about truth and loyalty, and about what love means, more by family nurture than by rational reflection, so we have in the Church a stored-up heritage of knowledge about God's ways and His will which is simply not accessible to speculation or mere rationality. It is the kind of knowledge which is accessible both to wise and to simple, with the advantage if anything on the side of the simple. For it is secured not first by reflection but by a kind of osmosis, by loyal and humble participation in the family life. This does not mean at all that the faith we find here and the love we learn here is exempt from rational handling: but reason is an aid in articulating it, not the condition of appropriating it. The Church in this sense is the primary *Gestalt* of revelation, as it is the primary *Gestalt* of grace, in so far as it is a community governed by the truth of

God in Christ, and a community which continues to gather men under the tutelage and governance of the same embodied truth.

And as with truth, so with goodness. The same community of faith which holds us accessible to the truth as it is in Jesus, holds us also within a community of loyalty whose loving compulsion overcomes our idolatrous loyalty to self, our partial loyalty to family and to nation, to class and to cause. It determines a "style" (*ethos*) of life which brings our divided loyalties and our conflicting mores into disciplined order, relating love to justice, compassion to truth, and all to Christ. It generates a life lived by loyalty rather than by principle: which avoids legalism by swallowing up law in love, and which avoids relativism by holding life under the absolute compulsion of the same love.

3. Every human family which cherishes its common life sets store also by some family *heirlooms*, items commonly of small cost or market worth, which yet unite the generations and remind the family of its origins.

It is not a full doctrine of the Christian sacraments to describe them so: but the homely symbols of water, bread and wine are this at least. They seal the unity of the Christian generations and of each and every generation with the Elder Brother and the God and Father of us all.

The seal of *Baptism* is the final witness against idolatry, and the final safeguard against every idolatrous claim, against the pretensions of race and class and nation. For it declares concretely and unequivocally that this child, this man, is a member of a redeemed humanity before he is a member of any nation, class or race: that he is a member of a community of brethren for whom Christ died, and that as long as men think greatly of Christ's death they will think greatly of this man's life. In its symbolism of burial and resurrection it makes the new humanity the fruit of the new birth, and declares that "the death of the self is the beginning of selfhood."

The seal of *Communion*, the bread broken and the wine poured out, is the sign that all are embraced in the new humanity, as all are ensconced in the love of God: and that not on condition of perfection, but on condition of acknowledged need.

4. It is the instinct of the human community, and specifically of the human family, to mark its solidarity by *festivals* of unity, in which the common life and its common joys are shared and celebrated. And so in the Church. The liturgy of the Church is primarily a liturgy of joy, in which the drama of our deliverance and the ground of our hope is recited, and the primal joy which is the purpose of our creation is recovered and declared.

It may be here that the contemporary Church is in most desperate case. The loss of the sense of the Church as the Covenant community, the dominance of the notion that it is simply a society for religious nurture, has thrown great areas of our worship into the most desperate confusion. The worship which should give to God the glory due to His name, which should celebrate in Scripture, song and story (which is what the sermon is) the mighty acts whereby God set His people free, has degenerated into a device for our own spiritual improvement. It has become a fancy worship, designed to provide an aes-

thetic and emotional charge, but having small relation, all too
often, to the profoundly joyous and profoundly serious business for which the Church is really gathered. It has become
subjective and individual, where it should be objective and
corporate. All kinds of "mood-molding" techniques have dis-
placed the hearty offering of the people's praise and prayer.
What should be a family festival has become a clinical device,
a kind of spiritual therapy which is self-defeating in so far as
it obscures the reality of the new humanity. For it is only in the
unself-conscious participation in the new humanity, in its
wholesome joys and salutary confessions, that the self is
healed of its bondage to the self.

5. Discipline in the Church has sometimes meant the right
of the hierarchy or of the congregation to reprimand, to impose penance, or to expel. Or it has been used to mean Church
Order, which is simply the responsible arrangement of the
Church's affairs in accordance with the Church's nature: the
valid appointment of its officers, the orderly conduct of its
business, the right functioning of its courts and assemblies, the
godly ordering of its common life. This last comes close to
what we mean here: for in authentic terms the Church's discipline (discipleship) is the plain and practical performance
of the family *duties*. And these duties are of two kinds, the
obligations which fall upon the members of the family in relation to the family itself; and the duty to the neighbors. The first
is church discipline in the strict sense, the second is the business of citizenship.

The corporate discipline of the Church is simply the Church
at its essential business of living like the committed fellow-

ship (the *koinonia*) it is, in the solidarity bred of the common
Faith. It affects not only the question of valid ordination and
good government, but the relation of the Church's members
each with the other, not only in spiritual but in material and
economic matters. To face the need of perennial, and therefore
of contemporary, reformation in this area of discipline brings
under scrutiny our racial practice and our economic behavior,
and all else that affects the life of the Church as a community
of faith.

American Protestantism is a perpetual riddle at this point.
It is not only the grosser failures of our congregations, as at the
point of race and segregation; it is the paradox of the local
congregation which is the ground of bewilderment. It is so
much like a church without a doctrine of the Church. The high
conception of the Church as the community of the justified by
which these pages are intended to be governed would be
strange news and foreign to a vast number of our people. And
yet how many a church-on-the-corner has the character of a
koinonia about it? It is easy to be ironic about the turkey-
supper and the general atmosphere of clubbery: and yet the
members of the Church enjoy each other, to a large degree can
depend upon each other, and contribute—even allowing for a
buoyant economy and an unexampled level of personal income
—in costly ways to the Church's maintenance and extension.
The question is of course how deep the unity goes, and how
inclusive it is. How often is it resilient enough to absorb a new
racial group? Does it transcend political differences, or does it
subsist by avoiding them? Is it a place where partisan and
party judgments are brought under the norm of a comprehensive justice, or does it move on a pious level where conflicts

of race and interest are muted rather than overcome? Still
more exacting: does it bring economic disparity into relation
to an *agape*-love in which "no man counted aught that he
possessed to be his own"; or does it simply take for granted
the inequities of an acquisitive society, tempered only by
stewardship or by a "tithe" which had meaning in an equali-
tarian society, but bears no relation to justice in a society such
as ours?

Nothing is more closely related to the integrity of the
Church than that it should set its common life at every level
under the scrutiny of the faith by which it lives, and submit to
the contemporary form of that perennial reformation which is
the condition on which it lives.

But the obligation is not exhausted within the family. "Good
citizenship is love of the brethren," and love of the brethren
includes our duty to the neighbors. In earlier chapters we
have tried to make connections between the community of
faith and the natural communities of men: the community of
justice for example, and the community of learning. The
Church is that community which submits to God's governance,
but that does not mean that He governs only where His rule is
openly acknowledged. The difference between the Church and
the world is not that God rules in the Church and does not
rule in the world: the difference is that within the Church it is
known under Whose governance we stand. But as to how the
claim of God to the whole world of His making is to be made
good: it is clear that this will be less by Church pronounce-
ments than by the penetration of the natural communities by
men who know their godly business there. They must know that
the service of justice is the service of God; that the integrity

and vitality of the Republic of Letters is a crucial Christian interest since all truth is Christ's from whatever source it comes.

The prime concern of the Church is with its own integrity rather than with its public influence. And yet the two belong together: for in the very measure of its integrity the Church must press home upon the wider society the meaning of the new humanity, and of human and Christian solidarity. There is a difficulty here: for the integrity of the Church, so far from being directly related to its public influence, is frequently in inverse ratio to it. The Church may be and has been at once dominant and decadent—and this has been true both in politics and learning. (It has also on occasion been decadent without being dominant.) That the Church should be at once integral and influential is beyond human contriving, an "impossible possibility" which in so far as it is achieved, is a peculiar work of grace.

To be a Christian, then, is not first of all to be a moral man, or a spiritual man, still less to be a Yogi rather than a Commissar. It is to be a member of the Community of Faith, the Company of the Justified Men. To be a Christian is to belong here: or rather, since this is in fact where all men belong, it is to belong here and to know that we belong here, in the new humanity which is the fruit of Christ's death. For here it is that life's sweet joys are sanctified, life's precarious decisions garrisoned by the divine wisdom, and life's tragic ambiguities neither avoided nor resolved, but comprehended by a divine forgiveness which is sufficient for our necessities, and strong in the measure in which we are content to be vulnerable.

To live *here* is to measure life not in achievement but in obedience, even if it be only the obedience of a sincere penitence: God be merciful to me a sinner. Here is the place where the power and the glory of God are seen, not in the Church's accomplishments but in the face of Christ. It is here that we learn, not only that the death of the self is the beginning of selfhood and the meaning of our salvation, but by what merciful mechanisms of grace the self is struck down.

A Note about Books

It seemed best not to weight this non-academic essay with a formal bibliography. Certain references of particular relevance are given in footnotes: but it may be of use to add here an informal note about accessible books which are germane to the argument of the successive chapters.

For the first chapter, on the Koestler-Greene-Warren material, sufficient reference is made in the text and footnotes to those other works of Koestler and Greene which are important in the main connection. Warren's novels are novels of quality, but *Brother to Dragons* is something of a break from his earlier preoccupations, and is not especially illuminated by reference to his earlier work. Aldous Huxley's *Grey Eminence* is essentially his account of the Yogi-Commissar dilemma, an analysis even more subtle than Koestler's of the complex connection between piety and power.

The interpretation of biblical faith which is set out very

generally in Chapter 2 has its best non-technical exposition, I believe, in the work of G. Ernest Wright. I have referred to his *The Old Testament Against Its Environment*. A more recent book of his, *The Biblical View of Man in Society*, is the product in part of ecumenical discussion and represents as closely as may be the growing Protestant consensus about the relevance of biblical faith to the corporate life of men. Wright's colleague at McCormick Theological Seminary in Chicago, Floyd V. Filson, has done work on the New Testament comparable to Wright's on the Old, in particular his *The New Testament Against Its Environment*. Will Herberg, in his *Judaism and Modern Man*, has provided a vivid interpretation of biblical faith in relation to the contemporary cultural movement. Herberg's work is of peculiar interest in that he himself is a convert from secularism and Marxism. Martin Buber's *The Prophetic Faith* is one of a series of momentous books by this most influential modern interpreter of living Judiasm.

I imagine that Chapter 3 is symptomatic of the influence even upon a Presbyterian writer of the present exhilarating revival of Luther studies. Anders Nygren's massive *Agape and Eros* (massive but by no means dull) has been followed by Philip Watson's *Let God Be God!* and many another.

Chapter 4 makes use of an essay by Paul Lehmann in the symposium *Christian Faith and Social Action* (John A. Hutchison, Editor). The symposium as a whole represents an American consensus—it includes essays by Reinhold Niebuhr, Paul Tillich, John C. Bennett, Will Herberg—about biblical faith and social life which is indebted both to the modern revival of biblical studies and to older traditions of social Christianity both American and European. Relevant also to

both personal and social ethics (that is, to both Chapter 4 and
Chapter 5) are the writings of Emil Brunner and Reinhold
Niebuhr. Brunner's *The Divine Imperative* is still the most
systematic modern treatment of Protestant ethics that we have
in English. For what it is worth I tell my students, bewildered
by the bulk and variety of Niebuhr's writings, that they should
start with one of the earlier exploratory works like *Moral Man
and Immoral Society*, then go straight into the systematic *The
Nature and Destiny of Man*, and then to one of the theologico-
political tracts like *Children of Light and Children of Darkness* (on democracy) or *The Irony of American History*. In
all this area of the frontier between doctrine and duty it is a
great shame that so much of Karl Barth's work remains untranslated, and that so much of it is intimidating even in translation. A. C. Cochrane of the Presbyterian Seminary in
Dubuque has recently translated Otto Weber's "report" on
Barth's writing to date, *Karl Barth's Church Dogmatics*. It is
simply Barth in a capsule form approved by Barth himself,
and it includes some of his previously untranslated work on
ethics. Paul Tillich's *The Protestant Era* is as important in this
general connection as any other single book.

There are almost innumerable introductions to *existentialism* (Chapter 6). Extremely useful are E. L. Allen's *Existentialism from Within*, James Collins' *The Existentialists*,
Kurt Reinhardt's *The Existentialist Revolt*. Any one of them
will give a sketch of the movement and sufficient introduction
to the sources. On one other main question, the relation of the
Community of Faith to the Community of Learning, the constructive work is in Walter Moberly's *The Crisis in the University*, and a succession of books somewhat in sequel to it like

Howard Lowry's *The Mind's Adventure* and the symposium *Religious Perspectives in College Teaching* (Hoxie N. Fairchild, Editor). This last is highly uneven but indispensable.

On the Vocation issue the present writer has a slim and preliminary book published in America as *Christian Faith and My Job*, and a theologico-historical essay in the *Christian Faith and Social Action* symposium. Robert L. Calhoun's *God and the Common Life* has been reissued to meet the present need, and Calhoun also contributes important material to the composite *Work and Vocation*, edited for the World Council of Churches by John Oliver Nelson.

In addition to the sequence of books by Daniel T. Jenkins (footnote, p. 170): the "high" doctrine of the Church which is in process of being rehabilitated in modern Protestantism is set out in *The Catholicity of Protestantism*, edited in Britain by R. Newton Flew and Rupert E. Davies and recently published in this country.